DEBT BUSTERS

MANAGING YOUR MONEY
THROUGH THE RECESSION

EDDIE
HOBBS

CURRACH
PRESS

Contents

Foreword

In 2004 I wrote my first book, a pretty slim affair that, to be honest, surprised its publishers and stunned its author by flying off bookshelves like water at a rave. *Short Hands Long Pockets* matched a growing demand for budgeting and financial management from those stuck in the middle in a boom economy – those who were not sharing in the vast wealth being created but muddling through with ever-higher costs and rising debt. Some of these ordinary, hard-working Irish families and individuals featured in RTÉ's television series *Show Me the Money*, illustrating what can be done with a will to succeed and a plan to do it. That essential truth hasn't changed but what has changed is the financial background of the country, with the advent, in 2008, of a full-blown banking crisis.

We now have far more serious levels of debt and a very large number of distressed borrowers, people who will never be able to make ends meet unless there are interventions that include debt write-offs. This book deals with budgeting to make ends meet, the Irish banking system, the property bubble that burst – and credit. It contains a self-help guide for the tough times ahead, whether you're broke today or afraid of being so, or worried about how to cope with debts repayments in the event of job loss or reduced income. Business owners who find their backs to the wall with struggling revenues, rising costs and banks belligerent because of upside-down property portfolios – where debts exceed values and rents fall short of repayments – should ideally hire an independent expert to present their more complex affairs to a range of lenders and negotiate write-offs. But if you fit the business profile, you'll still benefit from this guide as, in essence, the tactics are the same.

Hard to believe, I know, that Ireland could change so dramatically in such a short period of time. But if you look beyond the spin of government politicians and their political and business allies, the writing was on the wall for a property bust long before the toxic debt crisis hit Wall Street and infected world markets. The truth is that the Fianna Fáil government of 2002–7 blew the boom. Bertie Ahern's pro-cycle growth policies and budgets, presided over by Ministers for Finance Charlie McCreevy and (from 2004) Brian Cowen, stoked not just a property and credit bubble but general price inflation that jacked up business input costs. They also triggered a wage spiral, eroding the competitive edge that had fuelled the Celtic Tiger.

If you discount imported energy and interest-rate inflation it is clear that much home-grown price inflation came from the state sector, which was bloated by an additional 100,000 jobs. The public-sector pay bill nearly doubled – to €20 billion – not just because of expansion, some of it justified (especially front-line staff like Gardaí, teachers and nurses) but as a result of loony benchmark pay awards, a proliferation of agencies and layers of bureaucratic managers. Such was Bertie Ahern's profligacy and his courtship of the unions that today Ireland's public-sector wage and pensions bill exceeds average private sector pay by a considerable margin, whereas in an efficiently-run economy it should be the other way around, to compensate individuals for taking risks. By the end of Ahern's reign Ireland was pricing itself out of the game. That this situation coincided with a credit-bubble burst in the USA made matters much worse for us and was simply very bad luck.

Bumper tax revenues from the Irish construction boom masked the reality. Repeated warnings by independent thinkers were drowned out by the roar of the crowd and the pronouncements of economists captive to their banking and property employers. Much of the wealth created during this five-year period was an illusion, as we sold houses to one another in an ever-increasing borrowing and price spiral. All the markers were ignored and forty-year mortgages, capital repayment holidays, sloppy lending and irrational exuberance prevailed. The press and shareholders lauded the leaders of aggressive banks while the government and officials at the Department of Finance and the Financial Regulator stood idly by, intoxicated by tax surpluses. Inevitably the day of reckoning would come, when property taxes would be decimated by the next down cycle. But the costs of running the country would remain. The result is a devastating deficit in our public finances, worsened by the need to nationalise all or part of the banking system. This has raised serious questions about Ireland's creditworthiness and led to a deep contraction in the economy.

Much more important for you, conditions on the ground are changing at a pace unimaginable during the boom. Irish workers are facing the threat or reality of job losses and earnings are being slashed as employers remove the cream – bonuses, commissions, overtime and perks – and even demand pay cuts. Within one short year the whole nature and feel of the environment has changed. Lifestyles are in retreat, huge amounts of wealth have been lost and our standard of living is adjusting painfully. Forecasts of unemployment rising to one in every eight of the workforce are just part of the story. Those who lose their jobs are the most obvious victims of the colossal mismanagement of the last government but many of the remaining workforce have to service private debt that has ballooned out of all proportion, while facing cuts in pay and a widening of the tax base.

Despite the huge risks to Ireland, including the possibility of debt default if 2010 is a repeat of 2009, there are grounds for hope. Given the precarious nature the country's public finances and our inability to devalue our currency unless we abandon the Euro, we depend heavily on the global economy bouncing back fast – and that means the USA. At the time of writing, in January 2009, there are early signs of a possible recovery in the US and Europe during the second half of this year but much depends on an improvement in credit availability, an upswing in consumer confidence and the avoidance of a bubble-burst in US Treasuries which would hamper President Obama's ability to raise further borrowings. Fragile early indicators such as an increase in mortgage applications, an improvement in global freight and the doubling of cash build-up on the sidelines could yet prove the optimists right. Any fragile recovery led by the US will be preceded by six months or so of a sustained rally in financial markets where forward-looking analysts will detect an improvement in earnings forecasts by businesses throughout the economy – so watch stock market reports for portents of a recovery. I remain confident that the Obama administration will shift heaven and earth to get the US moving again. Then we will face the mother of all inflation cycles as the sheer scale of money printed to pump into economies combined with a return to rapidly-rising commodity prices, especially oil, will probably lead to double-digit price rises. It will be a time of great opportunities and even greater risk. But that's for another book.

Right now it's time to consider how to see your way through the Irish recession. This book doesn't contain any magic pills or formulas to make money problems disappear but it will give you lots of commonsense tactics you can use immediately. It will also give you an insight into the mindset and processes of the banking system that you will find very useful in navigating your debt-busting journey.

Best of luck

Eddie

1

A Brief History of How
We Got Here

The credit crunch is rooted in the US housing market and the level of toxic debt infecting banks caught up in it won't be clear until it bottoms out. It is hard to believe that US mortgage lenders could behave so recklessly as to give house loans to people who could never repay them and then sell these on, infecting the global banking market. But that's exactly what they did. So just how did we get to a point where confidence in banks is so fragile that many quoted banking behemoths face full or part nationalisation at the expense of taxpayers?

To help lift the US out of the Great Depression in the 1930s, the federal government came up with the idea of a home-ownership democracy. If they could find a way to allow people to own their own homes this would provide them with safety and security. It was a scary time as public revolt looked possible and the spectre of communism raised its head. Capitalism had collapsed with the exploding stock-market bubble in 1929. Millions of people lost their jobs as policy-makers erred by taking money out of the economy instead of pumping money into it.

In what was called the New Deal, money was injected into the economy and home-ownership was presented as the key to rebuilding the nation's confidence. Strange as it may seem today, up until then people saved to buy their homes and could only borrow the shortfall over five years or so. The concept of the twenty-year mortgage began with the New Deal. In Europe the notion of citizen home-ownership didn't catch on until after well after the Second World War, when governments began to think about moving away from state-provided housing and finding ways to encourage people to own their own homes. Ireland was late into the game, taking until the early 1980s to unlock the credit required to finance home ownership on a scale comparable with the US. We have since surpassed nearly every country on the planet in our rate of home-ownership.

The home-ownership concept worked well in the US, as the federal government came up with a scheme that insured banks against loan losses and provided the funds necessary to finance the enormous explosion in private ownership. That was until the Savings and Loan sector, the equivalent of our building societies – S&Ls, as they were called – began to find it difficult to raise money from depositors. The government relaxed regulations and the S&Ls began a period of reckless lending. This lax regulation fuelled a property bubble, an accident waiting to happen, and when it did happen, in the late 1980s, in excess of seven hundred S&Ls were closed down, the bail-out costing the US taxpayer more than $160 billion. Neil Bush was banned from banking for his role in the collapse of Denver-based Silverado Savings and Loan, which cost the US taxpayer $1.3bn. His younger brother George Bush left office in 2009 after passing a bill to rescue US banks in a crisis likely to cost the taxpayer ten times as much as its 1980s forerunner, the S&L collapse.

Securitised Lending on Wall Street

In the debris of the S&L crisis a few clever guys figured a way to buy mortgages from banks, package them and flog them to institutional investors like other banks and pension funds who were looking for a good return with lower risk. This packaging of debt and selling it on in bundles – called securitised lending – exploded in volume, as banks found ways of making the process cheaper. Banks and specialist mortgage-lenders offered home loans and almost immediately sold the loan on a low-risk basis to investors worldwide. Mortgage securitisation made sense as long as the lending was based on sound principles. This was until the invention of sub-prime mortgages: higher-risk debt sold to higher-risk borrowers. Sub-prime mortgages were packaged inside bundles of good mortgages, given a first-class bill of health and sold on to the marketplace for a truckload of cash, which was then recycled in more mortgages.

The US sub-prime market was helped along by government and Federal Reserve System (the US equivalent of our Central Bank) policy that encouraged lenders to relax lending criteria. Within a few years tens of billions of dollars were lent in an ever-rising property market. Moreover, many US consumers improved their lifestyles, not by spending their earnings but by refinancing their mortgages to release cash. To fund these billions, mortgage lenders once again used securitisation, packaging high-risk sub-prime mortgages and selling them off to Wall Street investment banks. The bankers knew full well they wouldn't stand a vampire's chance in sunlight of flogging sub-prime high-risk debt. So to get a good price they needed to have these mortgages independently rated as first-class risks. They did so by concealing chunks of sub-prime debt in portfolios of high-quality debt. Everybody was making lots of money – or so it seemed. Until house prices topped out, then started to decline.

It sounds nuts: lending to people who cannot afford to borrow and making it easy. But that's what US lenders did. They offered loans at deep discounts, reducing the rate for a few years and giving loans with capital repayment holidays, that is, interest-only loans. These stratagems reduced people's repayments to an affordable level, as long as there was income to repay the loan. Then to make it even easier lenders decided that people could certify their own income. After all, US lenders were interested only in *selling* the loan, as they could immediately lay it off to Wall Street dealers, who then sold it on to uninformed investors worldwide.

Inevitably borrowers' soft-loan periods expired and repayments dramatically increased. Matters were made worse when this coincided with a period of general interest-rate increases. The effect was to more than double many loan repayments. Within months tens of thousands of loans went bad and repossessions soared. It was the start of the credit crunch.

Straight away hundreds of top-rated 'low-risk' investments in US mortgage securities were downgraded. Within days banks around the world were reeling from the knowledge that billions in these investments had soured. They were faced with writing off incalculable losses. But their problem was that they didn't know which bundles of investments held toxic debt and which didn't. The worry quickly spread to the inter-bank market, in which banks lend money to one another, rapidly increasing borrowing costs and denying loans altogether to the banks thought to be most at risk. Worrying about bank defaults suddenly moved from being an academic exercise to being the main focus of financial markets. Inevitably, given the massive scale of exposure of Irish banks – especially Anglo-Irish Bank – to a declining Irish housing market, confidence in the stability of Irish banks, although untainted by investment in US sub-prime, began to ebb.

Throughout 2008 inter-bank markets slowed down as regulators and central banks made one attempt after another to unfreeze them. Tens of billions were made available as short-term debt to banks, encouraging them to lend money to each other. It might have worked, but then the troubles of Wall Street bank Lehman Brothers surfaced. Lehman Brothers was bankrupt and looked for help. But US authorities, fretting about 'moral hazard' – whereby if they bailed out one bank they would have to bail them all out – decided that Lehman's would have to be sacrificed. It was a catastrophic decision, with the same result as turning the water off during a fire in a nuclear plant.

2

Meanwhile, Back at the Ranch...

The effect of the near-collapse of the worldwide money markets, along with the problems in the US economy, triggered a global slowdown and a spiral into recession for many economies. The credit crunch, when it happened, denied money to all banks, including Irish banks. But the rot was already well in place before the Lehman Brothers' collapse during the tumultuous month of September 2008. The Irish economy was hugely leveraged to property and development sites, the values of which had been declining since late 2006, leaving Irish banks exposed at a time when confidence in the governance of banks was shaken to its core by the recklessness of US mortgage lenders and their Wall Street cronies. Investors in Irish banks were in no mood to accept blithe reassurances of soundness from bank executives or the Irish Financial Regulator. The game had changed. Investors, who had been warned for years of the risks posed by the property boom, rightly surmised that Irish banks had engaged in exuberant and reckless lending.

By 2007 the Irish public had grown nervous of buying houses at current asking prices, disbelieving the spin about a soft landing. The rot had started. Confidence was ebbing. The gigantic property bubble began to leak even more air. It was a slow hiss, barely perceptible at first. Builders were still building at a frenetic pace. Seventy thousand new homes were built in 2007. Except that no one wanted to buy them. The market had run out of steam. Worse was to happen the following year with three enormous shocks: a full-scale property bust, an international credit crunch and a strongly rising Euro.

In July 2007 the Minister of State for Housing, North Cork TD Batt O'Keeffe, used RTÉ's *Morning Ireland* to reassure listeners that the modest fall in house prices meant that timing was great to bail in. In a desperate attempt to get him to put down the phone, Batt's dog barked continuously in the background. Even the dogs in the street knew the game was up.

Early in 2008 business people throughout the country reported that the Irish economy had gone into a slump. Sales were falling, consumers were saving rather than spending, car showrooms were full of cars but empty of customers. The government, from early May under the leadership of Brian Cowen, listened, slightly tweaked its calculations for tax receipts, announced a modest cutback in spending and promptly went on summer holidays, exhausted by the never-ending farewell of former Taoiseach Bertie Ahern. Anybody with their eyes open knew Ireland was in recession. The ESRI think-tank finally confirmed it officially. The Lehman collapse on Monday 15 September started a run. Irish savers were rushing to take their money out of riskier banks. Finance Minister Brian Lenihan announced an immediate increase in deposit guarantee – to €100,000, one of the highest levels pledged by any government.

We were in for a ride few could have predicted. Just over a week later, on 30 September, Minister Lenihan was back pledging the wealth of the nation to guarantee all Irish banks after a run on deposits at Anglo-Irish Bank. Ireland had come within a whisker of financial meltdown. Had Anglo failed, so would Bank of Ireland and AIB. The minister's action staved off the collapse of the Irish banking system but at the time few realised the cost.

Nationalisation would be the next step. Before Christmas the Minister for Finance unwrapped a sizeable gift of state funds from the National Pension Reserve – €7.5bn, mostly as preference shares, paying an interest coupon of 8% per year to three banks. He intended to inject €2.5 billion each into AIB and Bank of Ireland for 25% ownership respectively and put up €1.5 billion for a 75% stake in the controversial Anglo-Irish, the country's third-largest bank. But on 16 January 2009, after revelations about the governance of the bank, Minister Brian Lenihan was forced to take Anglo-Irish Bank fully into state ownership.

Meanwhile Ireland's finances had deteriorated to the point where our credit rating was under threat and the cost of borrowing money had soared to more than 2% per annum above the benchmark German bunds. What happens next will become clear as the year progresses. The risk of having to nationalise AIB and Bank of Ireland remains high. The issue remains how we reduce our widening public finance deficit and sufficiently recapitalise banks – if bad debts mount above government forecasts – without going bust ourselves by being priced out of debt markets.

The Consequences of Leveraging

The use of bank finance to ramp up investment returns – called leveraging or gearing – acts like rocket-fuel in a rising market. On the ground the credit bubble, which was made ever greater by the magic of leveraging cheap money, has a very nasty downside. For new home-owners, even those financed at 100% of purchase cost, the equity immediately created in the home by the rising market instils a wealthier, feel-good feeling that encourages more spending and even more borrowing. Debt doesn't seem that important and anyway it's softened by the higher earnings and bonuses expected the following year, lower taxes and a boiling-hot jobs market. Everybody is geared to the hilt, including the peer group, so it feels safe. Understanding leveraging and resisting popular momentum when lenders are falling over themselves to sign you up is hard.

You heard property is on the up and up and rising by 20% a year. Your pals are already in the game: it's all they talk about. They tell you that if you buy today, you'll make 20% after one year. Thing is you haven't got €300,000, you have €20,000. But there's a banker poised to lend you the rest. Enter leverage. You borrow €280,000 and buy an asset you figure will be worth €360,000 the following year. You reckon you'll pay 5% interest on the loan (€14,000), sell the gaffe for €360,000, pay off the loan of €280,000 and interest bill of €14,000 and net a gain of €46,000 on your investment of €20,000 – a handsome pre-tax return of 230%!

But here's the story of the bust, what happens when values fall by 20%. Your property is now worth €240,000 but you still owe €280,000. Within a year you have recorded a loss of €60,000, which is costing €14,000 in interest to finance. That's €74,000 in losses or minus 370% on the twenty grand down.

That's the truth about leveraging: rocket fuel on the way up and on the way down

Like one in every two borrowers at the top of the bubble in 2006, Ciara and Frank Casey bought their home with a forty-year, 100% mortgage. They were delighted to qualify and considered the lender's approval and the mortgage broker's breezy advice as a testament to their financial strength. The purchase price was €350,000. The broker made a fast €3,500 and the lender expected to enjoy a fat margin of more than 1% per year on their debt for the next forty years while holding on to the deeds of the house. Nice deal: by the time they repaid the €350,000 capital they'd have paid the bank about €450,000 in interest. Ciara and Frank also borrowed €25,000 to buy two cars and used their credit cards to get a plasma television and pay for their two-week holiday to Egypt. Today their house is worth €250,000. Their cars are worth €10,000 at best. They owe about €400,000 and have negative net worth of about €140,000.

The Caseys are like tens of thousands of other Irish people. Nor is the loss of wealth limited to new home-owners.

Michael Cummins, a self-employed architect, bought three houses and owes a million Euro on them. The worst-case scenario, he thought, would be a soft landing, a temporary dip before prices moved higher. But last time he looked his houses were worth a lot less than he paid. Only one is now rented; the others he can't rent. He bought the houses thinking he could flip them – sell them for a higher price

CARLOW COUNTY LIBRARY

before any downturn. He has an interest-only loan and is subsidising the repayments from ad-hoc income and cash savings. Like more than 40% of his colleagues he's now without work and regrets concentrating his investment risk in the same sector as his earnings. But thousands of conveyance solicitors, builders, plumbers, quantity surveyors and mortgage brokers did exactly the same thing – and many of them are now jobless.

John Quirke has put ten grand a year into his pension for ten years. At the start of 2008 it was just breaking even with contributions. A year later it's valued at a third less than what he put in. His father, Sean, invested €200,000 in shares in AIB when he retired, on the advice of his stockbroker and after reading business journalists who had themselves invested in bank shares. His shares are now worth €20,000 and his dividends are gone.

Eileen Moore has €30,000, her life savings, with her credit union. Last year she was paid a €600 dividend that she used to fund Christmas spending. This year her credit union cannot pay any dividend.

CARLOW COUNTY LIBRARY

3

The Bubble Generation

Sean and Jean Donnelly live in an estate on the outskirts of a commuter town thirty miles from Dublin. They bought their home three years ago for €450,000, borrowing 100% from the bank. Both work in Dublin and they have a three-hour commute that sees them on the road every morning at 6.00 and home every evening at 7.00. Last year little Katie arrived. Her mother drops her off in the crèche on her way to work every day. Sean, who is thirty, is from Limerick and Jean, also thirty, is from Sligo. Sean is a scientist and Jean a marketing manager.

On the face of it they have a comfortable life. They drive two cars as Sean works in the city centre and Jean travels to Stillorgan. They have loans on their cars totalling €20,000 and credit card balances of €5000. Sean has been told his job is going as the company is downsizing. Within three months what little savings they have will be used up and Jean's income will be enough to cover only half their mortgage repayments. Sean's job is quite specialised and his chances of finding an equivalent job are very slim. He may have to move abroad or to another part of the country to get a similar position.

Sean and Jean have had their home valued at €380,000 but they're fearful that the valuation is unreal. Four houses in their estate have been for sale for the past six months at similar prices and nothing has sold. Their main concern is moving home. With a negative equity trap of at least €70,000 it would take a hefty increase in property prices before they would be at break-even. Should Sean get a job elsewhere, their chances of selling their home are quite slim. Even if they do sell, they cannot transfer their negative equity loan to their new mortgage.

Sean and Jean's debt problem is manageable but their ability to up sticks and move elsewhere is hampered by the fouled anchor their home has become. Their case highlights the need for innovative lending solutions from bankers. Ideally their bank should agree to transfer the negative equity to the new home.

The failure of successive governments to control land speculation around our urban centres through legislation, taxation and the nationalisation of strategic land banks led to a massive transfer of wealth from the Tiger cubs to a powerful developer elite. The controversial Fianna Fáil tent at the Galway races wasn't just a symbol of its political muscle but an open display of its hegemony. The harsh truth is that the generation of young people who bought homes at artificially inflated prices for the past number of years is now in hoc to banks with thirty- and forty-year debts, most of which are in excess of home values. Incompetent developers, who failed to diversify and kept rolling profits, doubling up into ever-bigger deals, have lost everything. Hundreds of billions have gone up in the funeral pyre. Developers will eventually find new ways of making money, the taxpayer is rescuing the banks, but the people who bought homes from 2004 onwards have been left marooned.

This is the debt-bubble generation, people typically born between 1969 and 1984 and today aged between twenty-five and forty. They grew up in the good times of cheap, affordable and abundant credit. They are the highly-educated, work-hard and play-hard Irish who considered credit a right of passage to tomorrow, a generation that willingly borrowed in the belief that the good times would always be with us and were prepared to put up with soul-destroying commutes and high childcare costs, as long as they could add to their prosperity.

The debt-bubble generation bought into the roar of the crowd, the never-ending self-congratulatory economic propaganda of government, the hubris of wealthy developers and popular media themselves addicted to property advertising revenues, that didn't ask enough hard questions and endlessly profiled Ireland's new property barons.

Not everyone could invest and there are those who were careful with their money, borrowing and saving wisely. But as the cost of living rose, the only way for many to keep pace was to borrow today from income to be earned tomorrow and refinance lifestyle loans into mortgages. Property was sexy. Anyone who tried to rain on the parade was labelled a loser, although it was always going to end just like previous property bubbles – in a messy heap.

As property increased in value people felt richer and behaved accordingly. Why should consumers rein in carefree spending and save for a rainy day when the government clearly wasn't doing so? Consumer debt soared to the highest levels in Europe and affordability was enhanced by low taxes, over-generous pay increases and lower interest rates. At the same time services and business increased margins as people thought little about price. Some sectors of the economy, protected by anti-competitive practices, made a bundle; public-service union chiefs negotiated soft one-way deals with a supplicant Taoiseach; and property developers, exercising careful husbandry of strategic land banks, hit the jackpot. It was Las Vegas on the Atlantic.

How could the outcome be anything other than an implosion, a collapse of the construction industry and the decimation of government tax revenues? We jumped from boom to bust, missing the soft landing promised by high-profile banking economists and others who had a vested interest in talking up the value of property. Within twelve months development land dropped in value by 60% and property prices shrank by a mind-boggling 40% in some areas and 20% on average. By the time property bottoms out prices may have fallen by 50% on average from peak to trough, allowing for inflation.

How much less severe would the fall have been without the global credit crunch? It's an academic question. The property bubble would have burst – the signs were there before the sub-prime problem emerged in 2007. By 2006 prices began to top out, with land accounting for up to 70% of housing costs in Dublin, starter homes priced at ten times the average wage and hidden borrowings for equity financed by credit unions. It was simply a question of how big it was going to blow.

Whatever the final outcome, one thing is absolutely certain: you'll need access to credit in the future whether you are refinancing your debts or looking for fresh funds. What is also certain is that the soft-lending theory is history, as banks revert to conservative policies, restricting credit in areas that were previously flush. Understanding how money works will help you to navigate the new marketplace in recessionary Ireland.

4

Banks: Like Them or
Loathe Them...

You, the Irish taxpayer, now own Anglo-Irish Bank and you might yet own the whole indigenous banking market, including AIB and Bank of Ireland, so it's useful to know how these (now) state assets work and why we had to save them.

The most important role of banks is the provision of credit. Banks literally create money. For every €100 printed by government, nearly €900 can be created by the banking system. By lending the money out and taking it back on deposit and by relending, holding back a little every time to meet depositors' withdrawals and cushioning loan losses, banks create money.

By creating money and lending for productive purposes the banks allow business to borrow to make goods, supply services, export, import and invest in growing business. This in turn creates jobs. Banks provide credit to individuals to buy homes, cars and other goods for which they would otherwise have to save. The combination of capital raised by businesses in the stock market and money borrowed from banks allows business to invest in long-term projects that would not be otherwise possible.

Banks also provide a safe place to store money, payments' systems and a range of services including risk insurance and export trade finance. Like them or loathe them, they are at the centre of economic development. Without banks modern society cannot function. Banks such as Bank of Ireland and AIB are so extensive and deep with their national networks of branches that they are embedded in society and systemically important. They are simply too big and too important to fail.

Banks get their money from two main sources. They collect deposits from the public through their branch networks and other channels such as the post, telephone and Internet. These are called retail deposits. For a long time this was the only source of bank deposits but over time an inter-bank market developed. If a bank had surplus deposits it would lend them to another bank. This system worked because government central banks were ready to provide deposits should a bank need them. During this period, banks loan-to-deposit ratio was about even. This meant that loans were financed by retail deposits, the cash coming in through the branches. Shortfalls in deposits were temporarily plugged by taking money from other banks in a national interbank market.

Over time the national market morphed into a world market as barriers to trade came down and technology and financial innovations allowed for twenty-four-hour trading in money in an interconnected global market. As the global economy expanded, the ready supply of wholesale money allowed banks to lend more and rely more on the money market to fund their loans.

The rise of the global money and capital markets meant that banks had a ready supply of cash and capital. This is what is called leverage, as the banks hold less capital per loan and finance the loan using a higher proportion of money-market funds rather than deposits. At the same time banks moved to reduce the amount of the their own money they would have to hold in support of a loan. Traditionally if a bank lent €100 the sum would have been a mix of retail deposits and its own capital. The ratios were about 75% deposits and 25% capital. But the level of capital has dramatically fallen to 8-10% on average and in some case as low as 4%. This has made bank lending riskier.

The banks' reliance on funds from money markets was revealed as their Achilles' heel when these markets froze in 2008 and banks were suddenly left short of money and couldn't raise capital. The price of raising money shot up and banks couldn't afford to pay the cost or refused to lend to other banks. Central banks stepped in and pumped billions of cash around, acting as the money market. Governments were forced to guarantee banks, hoping that they would start lending to one another again.

The lifeblood of banking is capital. It is the first line of defence against loan losses. If a bank owes more than it owns due to loan losses, it becomes insolvent. When a bank defaults it closes its doors, locking out deposit-holders but keeping their money. The administrator appointed will access the depositors' money to meet losses. Depositors will be given the choice of a discounted payout immediately or the full amount of their money back after a number of years. It's a pretty awful scenario – which is why national governments, quite apart from protecting the country's economy, are hell bent on avoiding it and why they put deposit guarantees in place to persuade people not to rush to take their money out of banks.

The Impact of State Ownership of Banks

As taxpayers we will be funding the banking bail-out costs for a generation. As a user of credit you should be concerned that you may not be able to borrow money on terms that are reasonable. Bankers will become far more risk-adverse than they should be. The effects of a credit crunch last for a long time after the crunch is over. One of the real problems with state ownership is funding the appetite of banks for capital. The evidence is that previous state banks were starved of capital, as states were too poor to finance their needs. The twin effects of government ownership and bankers becoming too shy of risk could stifle the credit needed by you and me.

Since the Second World War, banking crises have caused deep and prolonged recessions in which real property prices declined by 35% on average over a six-year period, economic output declined by 9%, unemployment rose by 7% and share prices collapsed by 50%. In 2006 the estimated value of Irish homes was €516bn, financed by €120bn of borrowed money. If house prices decline by 50% on average, Irish home-owners will experience a collapse in property wealth of at least €250bn – not counting losses in investments in overseas property. Remember that when an asset falls by 50% it needs a 100% bounce to recover its previous price levels. Even if the average decline is a third, the bounce would need to be 50% to recover – this is why it typically takes close to ten years before a bust property market returns to its previous price levels. Shares recover much more quickly than property but will do so only when analysts forecast rising future business earnings, which are invariably linked to economic improvement.

Apart from our collective loss of wealth in property and shares, we may yet have to finance a banking bail-out which could cost up to €30bn, depending on the banks' levels of bad debts, which in turn depends on the scale of job losses, the depth of the recession and the extent to which developers are bust. Over the next number of years the Irish government faces borrowing at extraordinarily high levels to finance the shortfall in tax receipts from the property and construction sectors that provided 30% of its income at peak. That's why the national debt, as measured by GDP, is set to soar from a trim 25% of economic activity in 2007 to a forecasted 68% by 2011. The real risk is that money will be difficult to raise in debt markets, that Irish government debt will be downgraded and that money will be rationed in future bank recapitalisation programmes, forcing Irish banks, quite literally, to shrink.

The creation of a 'bad bank' (most likely Anglo-Irish), to which the distressed debts of other banks are shifted, looks inevitable, ring-fencing the problems facing banks in raising sufficient capital to meet loan-market demand. If AIB and Bank of Ireland were freed up from having to nursemaid their bad debts with capital, they would have a chance to recover, replenish their capital base and avoid excessive shrinkage. When banks are forced to shrink, they severely ration credit and adopt heavy-handed tactics to pull in as much cash as possible. This exacerbates economic decline.

5

Understanding How Credit Works

At one time all we used was cash, the stuff we had in our pockets. We knew the value of cash as we could see it dwindle until the next payday. Computers brought electronic money, held in current accounts and accessible through ATMs. But we still used lots of cash and cheques. In the past decade we have become used to never seeing our money at all. It's transferred across computer data networks and paid into or taken from our accounts without us having to lift a finger. It's no wonder that lots of us never get a grip on how much we have or how much we're paying out.

Credit comes in many forms but falls into two categories: closed-ended – like mortgages and car loans – and open-ended – like credit cards and charge cards.

Closed-ended Credit

Closed-ended credit provides a fixed amount of money, usually for a specific purchase. The loan repayment is set over a specific period of time – hence the term 'closed-ended'. Typical purchases made with his kind of credit are houses and other kinds of property, cars, kitchens and furniture. The lenders are banks, building societies, credit unions and finance houses.

Closed-ended loans are based either on fixed rates of interest or on variable rates (also called adjustable rates). Fixed rates guarantee that you will pay the same rate of interest for the term of the loan, whereas variable rates will move up and down in line with changes in ECB interest rates.

There is a big difference in price between secured and unsecured credit. A secured loan means that the lender has an assignment over some of your assets, for example your home, or stocks or bonds. When security is provided to the lender this should be reflected in a lower interest rate than you would expect for unsecured credit. Short-term lines of credit such as credit cards and overdrafts up to certain limits have higher rates of interest because the debt is unsecured. Just because a debt is unsecured doesn't mean that the lender will not seek to recover the moneys owed should you default on the loan. An unsecured loan does not mean that your assets are not exposed to the lender; it simply means that the lender does not have a direct assignment over them.

Term loans, also called instalment loans, are the most common type of short-term loan. These are used to buy things like cars, computers and furniture and are usually unsecured. Payments are made monthly over terms like three to five years and interest rates settle somewhere between home-loan mortgage rates and overdraft rates. At the front end most of your monthly repayment is interest, and at the back end most of it is capital. Usually term loans can be cleared early by simply paying off the current balance but some instalment loans may charge penalties for early repayment.

Be careful of discretionary pricing. Some players headline their cheapest rate in their advertising but increase the rate sharply depending on your relative financial strength when you apply. Rates can range as high as 17%. (See Chapter 6 for more on the price you pay for credit.)

What credit unions offer is unique – a combination of reasonable rates, local decision-making and flexibility when things go off-track. Credit unions play a vital part in Ireland's financial marketplace and their mutuality and community-based ethos make their approach very different from commercial lenders when loans become distressed. Credit unions sometimes stipulate that you need to save for a few months with them before qualifying for a loan, but this requirement can be waived. Other unions require you to save while repaying debt so unless you want to save as well it is best to avoid these arrangements and push for a term loan only. Because of the strain of taking in so much money on deposit when interest rates fell after Ireland entered the Euro, credit unions need to lend a lot more and are well worth talking to. But always check the interest rates, which can range from a low of 5% to a high of 12% (See Chapter 6). Unfortunately the Credit Union Act 1997 allowed restrictive and anti-competitive market-sharing practices to continue that prevent you from dealing with a credit union outside your own area. If the opening times of your local credit union are inconvenient and the rates poor, check whether you can enter an affinity-group credit union through a family member.

Margin loans are available through stockbrokers, allowing investors a line of credit with which to buy securities such as equities and bonds. Typically margin loans are on a variable rate basis, a few percentage points above the cost of funds to the broker. Rates are usually linked to short-term government bonds or base rates. Stockbrokers provide this facility in order to encourage clients to invest more money in securities, setting the credit limit at up to 50% of the value of securities already held.

Service loans are typically used by insurance companies in Ireland but are also used by utility providers such as electricity and telephone companies. You can make payments monthly instead of annually, thus smoothing out the cost. Many people avail of smooth payment offers from insurers to spread motor and house insurance costs over ten months without ever checking the small print. These can be loan agreements with borrowing rates at up 15% and you'd be much better off paying the premium up-front for the year or even paying it out of a cheaper overdraft or one-year term loan.

As a general rule you should separate your source of short-term finance from long-term debt such as a mortgage, whether the short-term finance is working capital for a business in the form of an overdraft, or a credit card to fund lifestyle. Lenders regard loans as investments upon which they expect to make profits. When borrowers arrange their overdrafts, credit cards, residential mortgage and investment mortgages with one bank, the bank may attempt, in the fine print of loan agreements, to cross-secure all the debt against the assets held. Remember that the window to financial distress is your current account. In this a bank will quickly see a crisis unfolding. If a bank feels it's threatened it will close down your lines of credit. It therefore makes sense to arrange long-term mortgages with lenders other than those you use for short-term debt. Once a mortgage-provider receives periodic payment on a long-term loan it will be content and will have no access to information on the state of your current finances.

Open-ended Credit

Often called revolving credit, open-ended credit provides a line of credit that you can tap into and pay back on an ad-hoc basis. A range of providers such as banks, retailers, brokerage firms and other financial firms issue credit cards and provide you with a preset credit limit. Credit card interest rates are variable. Don't be misled by the headline interest rate advertised. The important figure is the APR (annualised percentage rate). In Ireland, just like in the US and Europe, the advertising of APR is a legal requirement. APR helps borrowers to compare bananas with bananas.

The rate normally moves only when there is a general movement in interest rates. Unfortunately the Irish experience has been that rate cuts have not been fully passed through to borrowers so credit card rates in Ireland are very high, typically in the range 14% to 18%. Remember that the cost of money to a lender in the wholesale market can be as little as 2%, so credit card debt, even in a recessionary market, produces fat gross profit margins to compensate for the inevitable bad debts.

You can use a credit card to purchase goods and services or to obtain a cash advance up to the credit limit. Credit cards require a minimum periodic payment that is calculated on the basis of your overall credit limit and the amount of your balance.

The best known provider of credit cards is Visa, which is a franchise operation that licenses different financial firms worldwide to offer cards under the Visa brand. This allows a franchisee to set its own prices and lending guidelines within the parameters prescribed by Visa. The market has expanded greatly, with credit cards now provided by retail stores, motor manufacturers and utilities.

Lenders use different methods to calculate interest but APR levels the pitch between different offerings. In open-ended credit the average daily balance is commonly used. This is calculated by adding all the daily balances over a month and dividing by the number of days in the month. This may or may not include new purchases made during the month. Some lenders prefer to use a combination of the current and past billing cycle in order to calculate the balance.

Don't ignore annual fees. These are flat fees payable for the privilege of using the line of credit. Lenders can charge very high fees on designer credit products, justifying these by the additional services they provide or by freebies such as discounts on hotel accommodation, free air miles or the replacement of lost or stolen goods. Some products provide emergency services for medical problems.

The minimum payment varies from one line of credit to another and can also vary on the basis of the lender's view of your creditworthiness. Hidden transaction fees may be charged, much like bank charges on current or checking accounts, by debiting money to your balance according on the frequency of usage. Late payment fees can be charged when you are a few days late with your minimum payment. Grace periods refer to the number of days given to you in which to make the minimum payment notified in your statement.

A mismanaged credit card is the gateway to serious debt problems simply because it's so easy to use and has low minimum repayment thresholds. Remember, all you have to do is to raise your arm from your wallet or handbag and swish, you've added another loan to your burgeoning portfolio. One in every two Irish credit-card users mismanages their card by not fully clearing the balance each month. It's an invidious system because even if you leave a Euro behind on your card, come interest-settlement day you'll be charged interest on the full debt. Let's say your balance is €5,052 and you write a cheque for a round figure like €5,050 – you'll be charged interest on €5,052 even though there's only €2 left on the card.

Charge cards, also called travel and entertainment cards, differ from credit cards by requiring the user to clear the total balance at the end of each month. The best known is American Express. Just as with credit cards you are borrowing money in the short-term to purchase goods and services and pay for them later. Typically charge cards have a range of annual fees linked to a range of benefits and services provided. Unlike credit cards they do not provide a direct spending limit: this is calculated by tracking your spending. Where users do not clear the full balance outstanding at the end of each month, a line of credit is provided at high rates of interest similar to credit cards.

A debit card like Laser is an electronic purse linked directly to your current account. There is no credit limit. The limit is set by how much cash you have in your account and any attaching overdraft limit you've agreed with your bank. If you use a debit card while in overdraft you're still borrowing, but at rates likely to be between 4% and 8% cheaper than most credit cards.

Debit cards transfer money from your account directly to the bank account of the firm from which you are purchasing goods and services. In time debit cards will not be exclusively linked to current accounts but will be pre-purchased by users for set sums of money to pay for things like telephone calls or to facilitate international travellers to meet the cost of travel electronically.

Overdrafts were the traditional gateway to trouble for over-spenders until credit cards with even more expensive rates arrived to replace them. You apply formally to your bank for an overdraft and it is attached to your current account. It is typically reviewed yearly but can be withdrawn at any time, especially if the bank feels you are over-extended elsewhere.

The overdrawn overdraft is probably the most con- tentious interface between banks and customers. When you go over the overdraft limit you break the contract with your bank. This doesn't automatically mean that your bank will refuse to honour your cheques but you will face surcharge interest of at least an additional 6% plus referral fees many times the norm. Overdraft rates range 9% -11%, so overdrawn borrowers will find themselves facing into rates between 15% and 17% plus referral fees.

If you use an overdraft always talk to your bank. Tell them if you're going to go overdrawn, and let them know how and when you'll clear the debt. If it becomes a hardened debt that you can't pull down swiftly your bank may suggest switching it to a lower-cost short-term loan. But whatever you do don't ignore your bank – keep talking to them.

Leasing

In 2008 the Irish car market was sucker-punched by the combination of carbon emission motor tax and the recession. Buyers deserted showrooms and the used car market was swamped, crashing prices. More than a million people drive cars and the market will rebound. But we put so much effort into changing cars and getting good deals that we frequently make a hash of the car finance. It's not uncommon, especially when finance is arranged through car dealerships, for buyers to confuse their lease or contract-hire agreement with a term loan. The two are distinctly different. Leases sold with bargain cars at an APR of more than 30% provide handsome profits for the car dealership in commissions paid by leasing companies.

The best way of understanding leasing is to regard an asset like a car as consisting of three parts: ownership, depreciation (loss in value) and interest costs when financing is used. When you use term loans you pay for all three parts and the vehicle is yours when the loan is cleared. With leasing you are paying only for the use of the car. You pay for the depreciation and interest but not its ownership, since you return the car at the end of the lease term. (With some leases you are given an option to buy the car from the leasing company at the end of the term.)

There are two types of leases, open-ended and closed-ended. A closed-end lease means that you can return the car when the agreement is finished. These are often referred to as walk-away leases. You do not have the responsibility of reselling the car but you do have the responsibility of ensuring that it is in good condition when you return it. These leases may limit the number of miles you can clock-up during the agreement period – if you exceed this limit you will have to pay an extra rate per mile.

Closed-end leases, while giving you the option of buying the car, allow the leasing company to sell it for whatever price they can get. An open-ended lease means that you carry the risk of the car's resale value when the lease is finished. Leasing payments will be based on an estimate of the residual value, the estimated value of the car at the end of the lease term. At the end of the term if the actual value is greater than the estimate residual value you may receive a refund. However, if it is less you may owe more money. This final payment is called a balloon payment.

The most common type of lease used in Britain and Ireland is the open-ended lease, which gives you the right to buy the car at the original estimated residual value. To distinguish these from other types of leases they are called lease-purchase agreements. Typically the lease is set up over three years or five years with thirty-seven or sixty-one monthly payments. The final monthly payment is regarded as buying out the residual value; in reality, the residual value is spread across all repayments.

Whether to lease a car or take out a loan depends on your circumstances. If you are (a) likely to do high mileage; (b) use a car that retains good residual value; and (c) you are unlikely to want to change the car, you should not lease. If, on the other hand, you are likely to do low mileage and may want change your car periodically, leasing is probably a better deal. Leasing also has the advantage of a flat monthly cost that cannot shoot with rising interest rates, which is a nasty by-product of adjustable-rate car loans. The risk in leasing is the possibility of wanting to opt out during the leasing term. The cost of buying out the lease can be more expensive than the value of the car, although this can be obscured when the leasing company provides a rollover lease, which means they offer you a new lease on the new car, rolling into it the buyout cost of the first lease. Particularly for people in business, there can be tax differences from time to time between the treatment of loan and lease repayments. You should check this out with your tax adviser.

How Does a Credit Institution Reach a Lending Decision?

Banks and other credit institutions pay close attention to the ratio between your liquid assets – such as fixed-interest securities, the cash value of life insurances or shares – and your short-term liabilities such as credit card debts and car loans. They will use a number of different financial ratios including the current ratio, which means your current assets divided by your current liabilities. Where lenders see that your current liabilities and your current assets are of equal size, that is a 1:1 ratio, they will regard you as a poor risk.

Banks look at the three 'Cs': collateral, capacity to meet repayments and character. It's a common error to believe that lenders love collateral above all else as in reality their first priority is your capacity to meet repayments on the debt. Banks will be also keen to learn how much you are already spending elsewhere on servicing debt and how much your lifestyle is costing.

Character is the next most important measure and this is signified by your credit rating. Lenders rely on the Irish Credit Bureau and their past experience with you to provide a rating. Credit bureaus measure whether or not you have exhibited good character in meeting repayments on previous loans and will score you accordingly.

Lenders will ask you for a formal or informal statement of affairs, akin to a balance sheet. This summarises the total level of assets and liabilities you hold. For secured loans they will seek collateral at least one ninth higher than the residential mortgage requested – that is, a loan to value ratio of 90% – and up to twice as much where the loan is used to invest in a speculative investment like shares. Banks will insist on higher cash down for people with occupations

they perceive as at greater risk in recession, reducing loan
to value to 80% or less as they price the risk.

Here is a typical example:

Two couples, John and Mary and Michael and Ann, apply for
a car term-loan of €20,000, repayable over five years. Both
couples have the same after-tax income of €50,000. The
only difference is that Michael and Ann have two children.

Clearly John and Mary have a lot of spare cash – this
is evident from their savings' account balance of €40,000.
Michael and Ann have a smaller balance of about €6,000.

	John and Mary €	Michael and Ann €
Net income	50,000	50,000
Less living expenses	(20,000)	(35,000)
Net available for loan repayments after living expenses (A)	30,000	15,000
Current loan repayments	12,500	12,500
New loan repayments	5,000	5,000
Total loan repayments (B)	17,500	17500
Repayment cover (A÷B)	1.71	0.85
Savings	40,000	6,000

But as Michael and Ann have two children their annual living
expenses are higher, at €35,000, than are John and Mary's
(€20,000).

Both couples are repaying the same amount every year – €12,500 – and are looking to finance a car which will cost them an additional €5,000 in repayments, bringing their total loan repayments to €17,500 a year. But when their ability to repay the €17,500 is calculated as a ratio of their net available income (after living expenses) the picture changes. John and Mary's net available income is 1.71 times their loan repayments but Michael and Ann's income is only .85 of their proposed loan repayments. This means that for every €1.00 in loan repayments John and Mary have €1.71 in available income (repayment cover) but Michael and Ann have only 85 cent. The banks will probably take the view that if they were to give Michael and Ann a loan the couple would be more likely to get into difficulties with their loan repayments than John and Mary.

Irish banks lent to far too many people in Michael and Ann's position without doing the right checks: hence the accusations of reckless lending. While 100% mortgages grabbed the headlines, among the worst culprits were car-finance firms and credit-card providers. The problem many people are contending with now is far too much unsecured or short-term credit, borrowed to finance lifestyle expenses.

Your Credit Rating

When you borrow from some (but not all) lenders, your loan is reported and recorded by the Irish Credit Bureau. The Bureau supplies your borrowing profile to its members, which means that if you get into difficulty with your loans this will affect your credit rating and ability to borrow again from one of the participating lenders. Not everyone is a member. For example, fewer than 10% of the more than four hundred Irish credit unions are currently affiliated, mostly because of inadequate technology – a matter that will be addressed.

Sharing of credit information and histories is reckoned to make lending more efficient, reduce costs and lead to more competitive loans. It makes sense for lenders to be able to assess risk more cheaply and quickly. One of the problems lenders have is that some borrowers tell lies or do not disclose all the facts of their financial history. The bankers' answer is credit scoring and using credit histories.

You can check your credit rating any time by contacting the Irish Credit Bureau (ICB), which offers an online service at www.icb.ie. For a fee of €6.00 it will send you details of your history. If you notice any inaccuracies you can arrange to have your record amended.

Your credit report includes:

- your name, date of birth and address (es) used by you in relation to financial transactions
- the names of lenders and account numbers of loans you currently hold, or that were active over the past five years
- repayments made or missed for each month for each loan (cumulative number where a number of months have been missed)
- the failure to clear off any loan
- loans that were settled for less than you owed
- legal actions your lender took against you
- whether any legal action is currently being taken against you

Your current repayment profile includes a twenty-four month log of your loans and repayments. This means that if you miss repayments this will show up for twenty-four months. Loan information is held for five years after a loan is repaid or settled.

The ICB report also includes what is called a credit score. This is a statistical estimate based on a number of criteria that rate your ability to borrow and your likelihood of defaulting on a loan. For more detail on how the scoring system works, see the ICB website.

Banks' Internal Credit Scoring

Banks use in-house credit-scoring systems to make decisions about whether or not to lend money. These take into account your income, job type, age, marital status and track record in saving and borrowing. If you do not keep up your repayments and hide from your lender, the bank's credit scoring system will refuse you credit the next time you look for it. Scoring is heavily influenced by the amount of debt you have at any one time. Banks are cagey about exactly how they these models operate but they are used to assess new loans and categorise existing loans from good to bad. Credit grading attaches a grade or code to existing account relationships. You may find that your accounts have been graded as high-risk and your loans considered delinquent. If this is the case you are unlikely to get any more money from the bank, which will report your account history and repayment performance to the Irish Credit Bureau.

Under its 'truth in lending' laws, US citizens are entitled to be given a clear reason why credit is being refused. This enlightened approach recognises that having a credit rating is like having a passport to affordable credit, without which people are marginalised. It helps someone with a poor credit rating to understand the steps they need to take to improve it. Unfortunately Irish banks are under no legal obligation to tell you why a decision has been made not to lend you money. Perhaps as part of the radical reform needed in Irish banking, legislators will address this gaping hole in consumer rights.

6

Practising Good
Credit Management

The best way to manage credit is to operate strictly within prudent ratios of debt and within your capacity to service that debt. In the case of credit cards and other short-term debt, ensure that you clear your balance monthly. If you have an overdraft, stay strictly within your overdraft limit. For medium- to long-term loans make sure that you give priority in your budget to repayment. The following are useful guidelines to follow:

1. Periodically find out precisely where you are. This means summarising all your assets and liabilities and your income and spending. When this is done calculate the cost of servicing your liabilities as a percentage of your income Ideally this should not exceed 33% of your net income: if it does you're heading for trouble.

2. Set a strict limit for servicing your overall debt as a percentage of your income. This is your lifetime limit. Ideally when you retire the percentage should be zero.

3. We all make purchases emotionally, whether it's properties, cars, boats or items like jewellery. Enjoy shopping around but impose a cooling-off period on your purchases. In other words never buy on impulse. Give yourself at least a week to think over any substantial potential purchase. Beware of sales techniques used to

get you to buy an item immediately or otherwise you
will lose the opportunity.

4. Restrict the number of lines of short-term credit you
use, ideally to one or two lines. Use of multiple lines of
plastic credit is guaranteed to get you into trouble.

5. Examine the different prices for different lines of credit
and always move to the cheapest lines.

6. Remove the temptation. Destroy your credit cards.
Write to the credit-card provider and request them to
take you off their mailing list to avoid repeated offers
of more credit.

When Big Bills Frighten You

Here's one of the secrets of budgeting that Credit Unions and
MABS champion – bill-spreading. You can do it yourself with
your own bank by setting up a budget-management account,
an account into which you regularly put some money and
out of which you pay non-standard bills. Examples include
annual car insurance, car tax, home insurance, school
fees and other periodical bills you know you will have to
pay when the time comes. The objective of the account is
to spread the load over a year rather than having a large
amount to pay in one month.

Have a look at this graph. It plots irregular household
bills across a year. You can see how amounts vary from a
high of €4300.00 in January to zero in May. The budget-
management account allows you to spread the cost of these
bills across the twelve months of the year, smoothing out
the peaks and troughs.

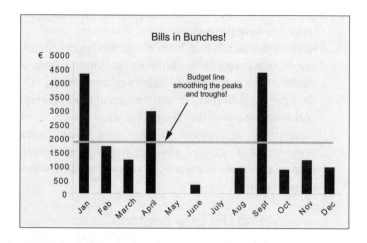

Here's what to do:

- Go through your bills for one year and identify the ones that arrive infrequently.
- Estimate all your bills for the next year. Bills nearly always increase so you will need to allow for slight increases.
- Once you have calculated the annual cost (be prepared for a shock), divide this amount by two.
- This is the amount you will need as an overdraft limit on the new budget-management current account you will open with your bank. That's right: you will need a separate current account and cheque book to make this work for you. The reason you need the overdraft is that some months you will be overdrawn and others you will be in credit as you move through the year.
- Once you've calculated the overdraft limit you will need, figure out what the interest and fee charges are likely to be, using a quick rule-of-thumb rate of 6% of the

overdraft limit. This is to allow for any overdraft interest charge you may incur on the current account. The limit you should look for is half the total amount, assuming your bills are spread throughout the year. Set up a standing order from your main current account, the one your salary is paid into, for one-twelfth of the total, and hey presto – you are up and running. The banks used to offer these accounts years ago but stopped as they were too expensive to monitor and control. There is nothing stopping you from setting one up yourself but be careful to track the usage closely.

To summarise, add back the overdraft interest and fee amount to the total amount, divide by twelve and there you have it: your monthly standing order to your new budget current account. Here's an example on the next page:

Annual Bill Budget-Estimator

Item	Amount €
Car Insurances	1400
Car Service	1000
Car Tax	1000
House Insurance	450
Heating	1500
Electricity	1200
TV Licence	150
VHI	1200
School Fees	7500
Golf Club	1200
Fitness Club	1000
Telephone	1120
Total Bills	18,720
Overdraft Limit (Total ÷ 2)	9360
Add Interest (Overdraft x 6%)	560
Total Outlay	19,280
Monthly Standing Order (= Outlay ÷ 12)	1606

Once you have worked out your standing-order amount, pop along to your bank to arrange your separate current account and tell them why you are doing it.

The Price You Pay for Credit

In the near or distant future, chances are you will back in the market looking for new lines of credit. Knowing a bit about how the market works may help you to navigate it better and avoid the mistakes of the past, like putting kitchen fit-outs on your overdraft instead of arranging a term loan, or paying for a driveway and landscaping for your home with your credit card instead of adding the cost to your mortgage.

Lenders offer many different credit products, changing the interest mix over time. Newer products replace older ones, some with a range of interest rates depending on the lender's assessment of the riskiness of the borrower. Lenders reserve the best rates to attract new customers and once you become a customer you are no longer new. Keep a close eye on the rate you are being charged on term loans as these can vary in accordance with your financial strength. One telephone direct lender has a spread of 10% between the cheapest rates reserved for the strongest customers and the dearest rates offered to the riskiest. Lenders will automatically charge their quoted rate unless you contest it.

Don't expect your lender to alert you to new special rates or discounts for new business. It is up to you to check these out: you may find you can switch to lower rates. You may have negotiated your mortgage at a standard rate but there may now be a lower standard rate. Don't be surprised. Many older mortgages carry rates that are higher than the quoted rate. That's why it is occasionally useful to check out the new-business market and whether competitors might make any contribution to switching costs. There's nothing quite like a letter from a competitor offering to take over your loan to focus the mind of your lender, who might otherwise ignore pleas from existing customers for improved rates.

All lenders are also borrowers. They are borrowing either from you when you save with them or on the inter-bank or money markets. This is the cost of money to lenders. They add a margin to cover costs and then their profit margin. The cost of money to lenders depends on the type of lender, their ability to manage their costs, the price of money in the wholesale market and the lenders' own credit rating.

So how can you tell whether or not you are getting a good rate from your lender? For starters, keep an eye on the European Central Bank (ECB) base rate. This typically decides the rate at which banks lend to each other. Under normal banking conditions this rate, called Euribor, is a tiny fraction above the ECB base rate. But the widespread distrust between banks at the peak of the credit crunch widened the gap between ECB and Euribor rates, dramatically increasing the coast of funds to banks. Consequently, reductions in ECB interest rates were not passed through to borrowers, except those with contracts stipulating that the interest rate on their loan should move in line with the ECB base rate. These loans became very valuable for borrowers, and some lenders attempted to fool customers to move into new contracts where the lender would earn a better margin – until discouraged by intervention from the Financial Regulator.

Your mortgage rate may be fixed for a period of time or for the entire loan agreement. A thirty-year mortgage may have a five-year fixed rate. This means that your repayments will stay the same until the fixed-rate period is over. When the five years are up you negotiate a new rate, which can be fixed or variable. If you do nothing, most lenders will put you on their standard variable rate, which may be higher than special offers they have.

Fixed-rate consumer credit agreements (loans and leasing) are fixed for the duration of the loan. Some agreements may allow you to move off a fixed rate and on to a cheaper variable rate. There may be a break cost to do this. Look at the savings you can make on a cheaper variable rate but factor in the cost of breaking the fixed rate.

Watch Out for Penalties

All consumer loans carry a penalty interest rate, which is usually charged on the unpaid arrears, on top of the normal loan rate. Penalty rates vary from lender to lender: the rate for a variable rate loan is about 7% and a fixed-rate loan 9%.

Take or example a car loan of €10,000 with €2,000 in arrears at a rate of 9.5%. €8000 is charged at 9.5% but €2000 is charged at 18.5%, which means the overall charge is 11.3%. If you are in arrears, the amount you owe is increasing at an exponential rate, far higher than the normal rate on your loan. You should get in touch with your lender immediately and agree a workout, if only to stop the penalty interest rates being applied.

Fixed-Rate Break Costs

If you want to break your fixed-rate loan and move to a cheaper-rate loan you may have to pay extra. Lenders will charge you the costs they incur for having to break their agreement with someone else to loan them the money at a fixed rate. The costs vary and the calculations can be complex at times. If you are thinking of switching, ask your lender to calculate the break costs, if there are any, and to explain how they arrive at them. Your lender cannot charge you a break cost for a fixed-rate loan of under a year's duration.

Credit-Card Interest Rates

Don't be surprised that these remain stubbornly high. Have a look at the rate your credit-card provider is currently charging you as an existing customer and the rate they are charging 'new customers'. The difference between the lowest and highest interest charge can be as high as 18%. At the time of writing the rates ranged from 2.1% to 21%, a gap of nearly 19%!

If you are a user of credit-card debt you should definitely shop around and be prepared to switch to lower-cost providers. Watch out for the 'extras'. You will be charged for any missed payments. Cash advances come at far higher rates. A host of other little additions make what looks like an inexpensive lunch into a Michelin-star meal at your expense.

Phone your credit-card company and ask them for a rate reduction or for their special rate. Threaten to move to a cheaper offer and mention the company by name, referring to the latest survey by the Financial Regulator or personal-finance journalists. If you don't get a reduction in rate, switch the balance to a competitor prepared to offer you interest-free periods for both balance transfers and purchases.

For years credit cards were considered transaction accounts and not looked on as consumer debt. Of course this view was promoted by card providers, who always talk about the numbers of people who pay off their balance every month. Credit-card debt in Ireland has increased faster than other debt because more people aren't paying off their balances and unpaid balances are increasing. Credit cards should carry a mandatory warning – much like mortgage offers that remind you that your home is at risk if you don't maintain your payments – but are currently not covered by the Financial Regulator's consumer protection code.

Credit Union Interest Rates

There are more than four hundred and forty independent credit unions in Ireland and they provide a vital role in the credit market, especially for people who find it difficult to negotiate credit with banks. As they are independent companies, each one is free to set its own loan interest rate, providing it is no higher than 12%. And they do. Rates vary from lows of 5% to highs of 12%. You may be one of the lucky people whose local credit union charges a low rate or you may one of the not-so-lucky people whose credit union is run more for its savers than for its borrowers and which charges rates of more than 10%.

Credit-union interest rates are a hybrid of fixed and variable. While the lending rates can be varied by the board of the credit union, they are usually left the same for a long time. The rate does not adjust in line with ECB rates. This is a hangover from a time in years gone when credit unions paid 6% on deposits and charged 12% on loans. The problem is, of course, that you aren't free to shop around for the cheapest credit-union rate. Credit unions are allowed to lend only to their own members, who must live within a certain radius of the credit union, be employed in the neighbourhood or be a member of an affinity group like the Gardaí.

Credit unions do operate what is called an interest rebate. Say they charge you a rate of 10.25%. Depending on the profits they make – which they call a surplus – they might pay you back some of the interest you paid during the year. Credit unions that use interest rebates generally charge more for their loans than those that do not. The problem is that you may be charged the higher rate and not be paid a rebate. Some credit unions charge an interest rate at the full legal limit of 12%. If there is a rebate tell your credit union to pay it into your loan account, not your savings account. As a member of the union you are a shareholder so you should take an interest in its affairs. Write to the board or attend the annual AGM and ask your credit union to ditch interest rebates and lower the rate instead. This way the credit union will start working for borrowers as well as savers.

7

Determining the Degree
of Your Debt Problem

Money doesn't come with a set of instructions, so getting into financial difficulty can be a very confusing and frightening experience. You don't know what to do or where to turn. You feel you can't talk to family or friends because they will consider you a failure. Your pride and embarrassment act as a barrier to accepting the scale of the problem. You feel like running away and hiding.

These feelings can be so overpowering that denial of debt is one of the biggest problems people have to contend with. Fear of the unknown, the fight or flight response, brings on stress that can cause a paralysis of thought and action. It can set up a negative spiral of thinking that persuades you that money problems will go away, a spiral that you can break out of only by taking positive informed action today.

The tactics in this book are for anyone who has problems with debt, whether it is a feeling that you could do better, a bigger problem that sees you are struggling to make repayments or a really serious problem where you are so snowed-under that debt collectors are threatening to drag you into court.

You are not alone and there is nothing wrong with having financial problems. Tens of thousands of people have had problems in the past and have resolved them, returned to financial health and got on with their lives.

Tens of thousands have recently joined the ranks of people with financial problems not because of anything they did wrong but because of circumstances over which they had no control. You can work through what is a temporary problem that will one day be no more than a bad memory.

Most people who have financial problems have gone through a life-changing event. They may have lost their jobs, had their hours of work reduced, their bonus or commission-income slashed, they have become separated, divorced or lost a partner. People get ill and cannot work. Some people have good jobs and respectable income but for some reason cannot control their spending and borrow large amounts to finance day-to-day living. You may be one of the many who were mugged by the recession and are experiencing financial problems for the very first time through no fault of your own.

Follow the steps outlined in this book. They are tried and tested. People who take positive action can solve their financial problems in a way that makes them feel more in control. They feel safer and can live their lives in peace. If you have a debt problem, the chances are that you do not feel safe or secure. You may feel crushed, totally at a loss about how to get out of the hole. Worse still, you may have feelings of depression, or even despair. Being seriously worried about debt can really hurt you psychologically and physically. That's why this book also deals with recognising depression and what to do about it (see Chapter 16).

A combination of not really understanding the condition of the balance sheet and cashflow and the very human tendency to stick our heads in the sand prevents us from dealing with our money problems. Denial is a very real issue, as the following story illustrates:

In November 2008 a business supplier asked me to talk to a another businessman who'd shared his money worries with his long-time friend. Like many others, this businessman had diverted his excess income into aggressively building up a property portfolio. He was indirectly linked to, and dependent on, the property and construction marketplace. This sounded familiar but it wasn't a great starting-point as the businessman hadn't come to me directly for help. Eventually we made contact and, after receiving an inadequate summary of his position, I emailed him a layout to complete that would capture property values, outstanding debt, rents, loan repayments and the financial position of his company so that I could look at supporting cashflows and financial accounts. I needed to see the complete picture, warts and all, before I could devise a plan for negotiating with the bank.

After several days the businessman sent me a summary portfolio of about fifteen properties acquired since 2004 and financed by four different banks. The data was full of holes. Some bank debt was not recorded, some rents were included as expectations rather than real income, there were uncompleted new builds in a remote rural village he expected to sell because the local auctioneer said he would, and the valuations provided looked distinctly odd. A quick piece of research revealed that the values were still showing 2006 prices. The businessman, who at this point had borrowed over €5 million, wasn't yet capable of facing the truth in private, never mind revealing it to an independent adviser. Three weeks and several emails later a clearer picture was emerging of debt well above values, rents well below loan-servicing costs and a business operating on a pulse of income, having shed most of its workers. But even at this point the valuations were inflated. This businessman was in a state of denial, engaged in the entirely fruitless exercise of hiding his problems from himself by creating false financial summaries.

This man was not yet ready to be helped. He had not accepted reality and will only do so when the situation is closer to being irretrievable. It was also clear that both he and his wife – who administered the business – had a poor grasp of their own balance sheet. Just how they had managed such complexities, continuing to borrow and adding further concentrated investment risk to their portfolio – and how the banks continued lending to them – is the classic story of the Irish credit bubble. By the time the dust settles they'll be lucky to hold on to the family home and the business. The banks will tear his balance sheet apart.

The remedies you need to consider depend on the level of money distress you're in. You may be able to adjust relatively easily with a commonsense change of direction in lifestyle or you may need to put together a presentation to your bankers to kick-start the renegotiation of your debt. One way or another, there's always a plan. There's always hope and you need to begin by determining the degree of your debt problem.

Mild Debt

Kieran Nugent works for a large company and while there is no threat of his losing his job and he's on a good salary of €65,000 a year, he has a feeling that he hasn't as much money to spare as he used to have. He's been caught short coming up to payday and using his credit card more and more to pay for larger bills such as car insurance.

You will know that you have a mild debt problem like Kieran if:

- you feel the strain of debt and find that every month there is little left over to save.
- you increasingly pay larger bills with your credit card.
- you wonder why your current account is always in the red and your interest charges have increased.
- you face a hefty drop in income as your remuneration package has been cut or you're facing redundancy.
- you need to borrow to fund a child's education or change the car.

If you're spending a bit more than you earn, financing your lifestyle by using short-term debt such as credit cards and bank overdrafts, this will be your situation.

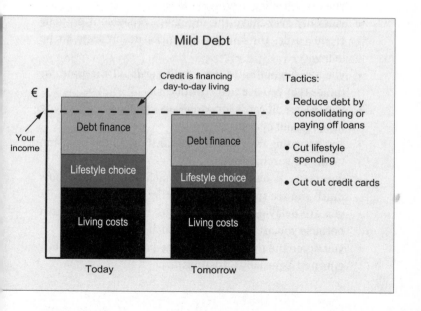

Heavy Debt

Mary and Pat Dunlea have been worried about their financial situation for nearly a year now. Mary's auctioneering business has collapsed. Pat can't reach his sales targets and his commission is down nearly 80% on last year. They realise that they must cut back on their lifestyle expenses and take a hard look at their investments and debt. Right now they are maxed out on their credit cards, their overdraft is at the limit and their unpaid bills are mounting.

You may be in a similar situation to Mary and Pat if:

- an increasing percentage of your income is going to servicing debts.
- you are beginning to juggle your lines of credit, delaying payments on some lines and paying others.
- you are receiving overdue notices.
- you only ever make the minimum repayment on your credit cards. Outstanding balances never seem to be falling.
- you are beginning to use credit cards all the time for things that you use to buy with cash.
- you use credit cards for essentials like food because you have run out of cash.
- you are going over your overdraft limit all the time and incurring surcharges.
- you never know exactly how much you owe and how much you are spending on servicing debt.
- you are delaying vital visits to your doctor and dentist because you are afraid of how much it will cost you
- you dread the thought of birthday parties, having to buy gifts and especially Christmas.

- you worry about your overall level of debt. All the time.
- you are beginning to hide your bills from yourself, sticking them into a drawer and refusing to open them.
- you are increasingly using new lines of credit to pay for old lines of credit.

If you're spending a lot more than you earn, financing your lifestyle by short-term debt such as credit cards and bank overdrafts, your situation will look like this:

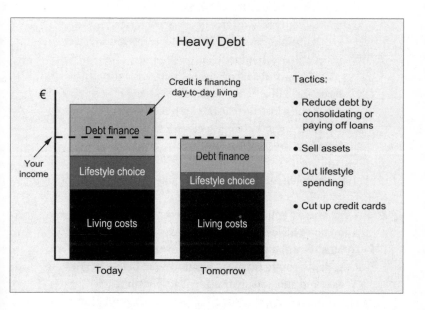

Distressed Debt

Liam and Róisín Fitzgerald have a hefty mortgage of €600,000 on their own home and investments in three buy-to-let properties. With combined loans of €900,000 they are under severe strain, as their cashflow is far less then their outgoings. Two of their rental properties have been vacant for the past three months and their loans are in arrears by the same period. They have two car-loans of €35,000 and combined credit-card balances of €30,000. Liam was made redundant three months ago and as he had worked for his company for only two years his severance package was a mere six months' salary. Róisín is a self-employed architect and has only one contract in the pipeline.

Their overdraft limit has been withdrawn and their main banker has written to demand that they bring their arrears on their home loan up to date. Last week they received five letters from four different lenders and a debt-collection agency.

You know you have distressed debt like the Fitzgeralds if:

- you are in a spiral of debt that increases every month and you don't have the income to make your repayments.
- you have unlet property in non-prime locations.
- the rents you're taking in are now well below borrowing costs and subsidising the gap is impossible.
- your business or earned income has fallen below your ability to service debt.
- your debts now exceed the combined value of your property and the banks are demanding extra security.
- you are struggling to make ends meet and even paying the ESB bill is a problem for you.

- sometimes you're so out of cash you hardly have enough to put petrol in your car.
- your credit is gone, limits have been exceeded and solicitors' letters are now arriving.
- banks are beginning to lose patience with you.
- you're living on social welfare, having lost your job or livelihood.
- your creditors are circling, all vying for their pound of flesh.
- you've already burned up your liquid assets to support your position and pared personal spending to the bone.

If you are living hand to mouth and your debts are simply non-repayable, a graphic of your situation would look like this:

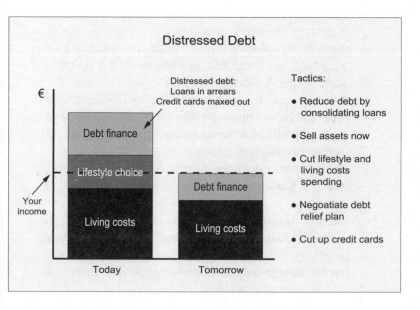

Especially if you have distressed debt, try not to give in to despair and lose your courage. Many people have been there before you, lived through it and bounced back at the next up-cycle. Wherever you're starting from, below is a list of remedies and tactics that will help. How many of these you will need to adopt will depend on how deeply in debt you are.

Remedies for Mild Debt Problems

1. Run a cash diary for a few weeks to record where you are bleeding cash.
2. Add the results to your electronic spending to determine overall spending (See Appendix 1 for a budget format).
3. Ruthlessly separate all spending into necessary and optional.
4. Repeat Step 3 at least five times and be honest. Your ESB supply is necessary: skiing isn't.
5. Look for efficiencies: things you can cut down or give up altogether. Booze and fags commonly eat up 10%-20% of after-tax income.
6. Change your shopping habits. Buying from Lidl and Aldi and local fruit, vegetable and meat vendors can save you 16% on your shopping bill, according to the National Consumer Agency.
7. Deduct necessary spending from after-tax income: the result is how much you can allocate to optional spending.
8. Do up a financial snapshot, listing all your loans. Begin with the loan with the highest interest rate. Your mortgage will be at the bottom of the page, store and credit cards at the top.

9. Consider how you might consolidate the most expensive debt with the least expensive further down the page. (see Chapter 8). It is easiest to consolidate with a lender with whom you haven't missed repayments. Ideally consolidate with a term loan you can afford. If you add to your mortgage, commit to clearing the extra amount borrowed within a few years by accelerated repayments.

10. Get your record at the Irish Credit Bureau and insist that lenders correct any mistake on your file

11. Set a monthly budget and stick to it. Compare actual with budgeted spending for the next year.

12. Use a budget management account for your big, in-frequent bills (see Chapter 6).

13. Don't lose focus and slip back into spending without thinking.

14. Cut the top off your credit card horizontally, so you can use it for on-line cheap flights but not for day-to-day shopping. Make sure not to cut off the security code that is usually printed on the signature strip.

15. Resolve to spend money only you have in cash in the bank, using cash cards.

16. If it helps, set up a budgeting account with the local credit union to pay for utilities and rent.

17. Set a positive goal for yourself a few months ahead as a reward for getting back on the straight and narrow.

18. Share your plan: tell your family and close friends what you're at so that they'll support you.

Extra Remedies for Heavy Debt and Distressed Debt

These are within a whisker of each other and both require you to renegotiate terms with the lending market. However, in the case of distressed debt, full or partial write-offs will be needed. Each procedure begins with your preparing a statement of affairs, a detailed summary of your assets and liabilities and of your income and expenditure. These are the documents you will be presenting to lenders, so be honest. Nothing queers the pitch and raises the ire of lenders faster than catching someone withholding something materially important.

This exercise in assembling a debt proposal is about biting the bullet, acknowledging one of two facts: either you cannot carry your debts without radical restructuring or you will never carry them no matter what restructuring is agreed, unless some debt is written off. Look at it from the lender's perspective: you can't squeeze blood from a stone and pursuing legal remedies is hugely costly. Your job is to make a proposal that's cheaper than legal action, with a better net outcome for the lender. You can only make your case convincingly if you are ruthlessly honest.

1. Prepare a detailed balance sheet, a financial snapshot of what you own (assets) and what you owe (liabilities). See Appendix 2 for a completed example.
2. Keep the summary simple, beginning with your most liquid assets like cash, life policies, post office saving certificates and shares. Continue to your least liquid assets like property.

3. Support the figures, especially your debts, with back-up schedules outlining the rates, costs and terms of your borrowings.

4. List your sources of earned and unearned income and adjust if a downturn is definite.

5. Prepare a spending budget. The lender will want to see you rein in your personal expenses if they're to support your proposal.

6. Aim to sell all liquid assets to clear out the most expensive debt. There's no point paying 18% on credit-card debt while you have money in a life policy averaging 5% per annum. But keep a cash reserve of at least three months' lifestyle costs separately.

7. One possibility is to use a lump sum to negotiate loan settlements. Lenders might agree to write off your loan if offered a lump sum to settle. See the distressed debt proposal in the Chapter 9.

8. Consider what other belongings can be liquidated. Clinging to yachts, racing cars, helicopters, unencumbered property or financial assets when faced with legal action for debt recovery makes no sense.

9. Use e-bay to sell surplus consumer stuff you've acquired but never use.

10. Check your credit rating. It's probably damaged and you will need to plan to repair it.

11. Make sure your tax affairs are in order. If not, list the Revenue as another debtor. Check for any tax refunds due or unclaimed allowances.

12. Would any of your lenders consider a consolidation proposal after you've taken these steps and committed to a budget for the next few years? If you think they

might, approach them with your plan and your request for a consolidated loan.

13. What about extending the term of a loan to reduce current repayment costs?

14. Would any of the lenders consider switching from capital and interest repayments to interest only? If there's no room for consolidation or restructuring, the way forward is to determine your repayment capacity. Remember that the objective here is to calculate authentically how much you can afford to allocate to debt repayments. Your aim is to put yourself on a more equal footing with the lender's agent, who is trying to get you to repay the loan in full. You now have the facts and nothing they can do can worsen your position, saving the forced sale of your home. Don't ever approach lenders with a plea: approach them with a plan.

8

Consolidating Debts

Anne Myers is a teacher. Over the past three years she has run up short-term debt of €28,000. She has €5000 in savings. Anne hasn't yet taken the plunge and bought a house and is quite happy to rent.

Purpose	Owes €	Rate
Car Loan	10,000	10%
Credit Cards	15,000	18%
Overdraft	3,000	10%

Anne has completed her budget and knows how much a month she can afford to repay. She has taken the following actions:

1. She used her savings to pay €5000 off her credit-card account, reducing it to €10,000
2. She applied to her bank for a five-year debt-consolidation term loan, amalgamating her car loan, credit-card balance and overdraft into one loan.
3. She agreed to keep a credit card with a reduced credit limit and the balance will be cleared in full from her salary once a month.
4. She has undertaken to keep her current account in credit.

5.   She will also save €300 per month by implementing this plan.

In five years Anne will have paid off her loan. This means she cannot change her car but she says she will drive it into the ground. The fact that Anne took action and did up her budget gave her the confidence to apply for the loan. Anne applied one of the golden rules in debt consolidation: she restricted her access to the high credit limit that got her in the soup the first day. During the boom lots of people saw their credit-card limits as targets rather than limits!

Martin and Frances Tyrrell

Martin expects to lose his job and go on jobseeker's benefit. Frances works as an IT project manager and earns €90,000 a year. They have two children aged seven and eight, who attend the local primary school. Their mortgage is €250,000 and they have a car loan of €25,000, along with combined credit card balances of €15,000. Their savings are small at €5,000 – mainly children's allowance saved over the year. Last year they improved their home, which cost €25,000 from their savings. Martin will get a redundancy payment of €15,000. Rather than muddle through, Martin and Francis plan have drawn up a plan:

Purpose	Owes €	Rate
Car Loan	25,000	9.5%
Credit Cards	15,000	18.0%
Mortgage	250,000	3.95%
Savings	5,000	2.0%

Martin realises that finding a new job may be quite hard and take a long time. While Frances thinks her company may also announce job cuts, she believes her position is quite safe. They have carefully considered their budget and realise that without Martin's income they will be stretched to make repayments on their loans. Last year they invested their SSIA savings in home improvements. Their home was worth €600,000 in 2007 but they reckon it is now worth far less and that its value may fall to €400,000 by the end of 2009. With a mortgage of €150,000 they have a reasonable cushion of equity they may be able to borrow against. They took the following action:

1. They completed their household budget, factoring in the drop in Martin's income and allowing for savings in after-school child care now that Martin is at home.
2. They identified savings of €1000 a month, mainly in the areas of cars and entertainment.
3. They want to keep their savings going as they feel this is a good means of funding their children's education. They are saving and not spending the children's allowance.
4. They applied to their bank for €40,000 as a top-up loan to their mortgage, saying that it was for debt-consolidation because Martin was temporarily unemployed. They committed to eroding this extra €40,000 from their mortgage account over five years, which will be more realistic for them once Martin finds a new job.
5. Their bank has agreed to the additional loan at a rate of 3.95%.

6. Frances and Martin's monthly repayments have dropped from €2580 to €2150.
7. They got rid of one credit card and now have a joint card with a reduced limit which will be cleared monthly from their current account.

In both these cases it made sense for the people involved to consider consolidating their debt into one more affordable loan. The key is that both parties have reasonable jobs and reliable income. The golden rule, once the bitter medicine is beginning to work, is not to borrow up again.

Debt consolidation should be a last resort to be used with care, as frequently you will end up paying off loans over a far longer term than you had originally planned. Having consolidated their loans, many people fall into the trap of starting to borrow again. Stories abound of people who financed their day-to-day living by using the equity in their homes as a form of cash machine – and not just in the United States.

9

Preparing

a Distressed Debt Proposal

A debt proposal with balance sheets and budgets is the best bulwark against the loss of your home. Before you present your proposal you should run it by an experienced debt counsellor or independent expert who will be in a position to spot any flaws in your presentation and, if necessary, improve it.

Simply clarifying your position in detail, beginning to take some action and putting a plan on paper helps confidence no end. It beats the hell out of sticking your head in the sand and not truly knowing the details of your affairs. But at this point the tricky task of coming to some arrangement with your creditors begins. This will require patience and forebearance in the face of robust counter-tactics by some creditors.

You may be broke and not have the income to make your full repayments. You may be in substantial loan arrears with letter after letter arriving from your lenders. You may be threatened with legal action. You may be on the Dickensian treadmill of the legal debt-collection process. But there is a way out. The key is to propose a debt repayment plan that you can afford and that your lenders will have no option but to accept. The alternative for them is to incur legal costs pursuing you in the courts, only to have to write off the loan eventually. Your repayment proposal may take the form of reduced repayments or interest being suspended for a period of time, after which the balance is written off. It may take the form of a debt-consolidation loan to repay other borrowings in full, or a reduced settlement figure agreed by both parties.

Use an experienced debt negotiator if you feel over-whelmed by the prospect, but you may be surprised by how straightforward the process is once it commences. Remember, lenders much prefer well-prepared solutions to chasing defaulters for many months. It's less hassle and saves a ton of money – money that would be lost anyway either by default or in legal fees and valuable management time, especially given the current very large number of distressed borrowings in Ireland.

You must be realistic and honest in what you propose. Don't promise something you know you can't deliver as a ruse to buy time. You may hope things will get better but is that really likely?

1. Prepare your spending budget.
2. Do up your cashflow projection.
3. Decide how much you can afford to repay each month in total, that is, your repayment capacity.
4. Match your repayment capacity to your debt.
5. Seek professional help if you need it. Don't be proud. You have a serious problem that you need help with *now*.

How to Prepare Your Financial Snapshot

The essential starting-point in any remedy is a complete snapshot of your position, a document in which you list what you own and what you owe. It will normally take about an hour to complete. Appendix 2 contains a blank format or you could construct your own version either on paper or on your computer. There isn't a killer template; the important thing is to prepare the snapshot well and adjust it to fit your affairs

Get the paperwork together for all your financial assets – the things you own – include savings, deposits, insurance bonds, share certificates, shares and pension funds. If you can't find the paperwork, don't worry. Contact the asset manager or bank and order a statement. What is important is to think of everything. If you're unsure of a value, take a stab, an educated guess: you can always validate it later.

The next thing is to find the most recent information on everything you owe. You should get together all your credit card bills, mortgage and current-account statements and any car finance, leasing or other loan agreements. Your current balance will be on your latest statement, which should also include the interest rate you are paying. Put all these documents in one file. Don't forget the small loans, even loans from family and friends and zero-interest loans that don't need to be repaid until next year. Leave nothing out, including personal guarantees you've signed.

If you don't have your loan agreements, ask for copies to be sent to you. Lenders are legally obliged to provide you with these copies. Most of your loans will have a regular repayment schedule, either weekly or monthly. If you are making quarterly or half-yearly payments, adjust these for monthly amounts.

One way to establish your existing repayments is to check all the direct debit and standing order payments on your main bank account, usually a current account. Here's an example:

What I Owe Credit Provider	Balance Owing €	Term Remainin (years)
Mortgage	300,000	30
Credit Card	20,000	
Bank Term Loan	12,000	3
Car Lease	20,000	4
Credit Union	10,000	6
Overdraft	5000	
Tax Liability	10,000	
Total (a)	377,000	
What I own Liquid assets	Balance or Value	Term
Bank	10,000	Demand
Building Society	15,000	3-month fixed
Tracker Bond	20,000	
Shares	1000	
Total (b)	46,000	
What I own Fixed Assets	Value	Net Equity
House	350,000	50,000
Cars	20,000	(5000)
Investment Bond	25,000	
Pension Fund	110,000	
Paintings	5000	
Boat	10,000	
Total (c)	520,000	
Net Assets		
Total (b) + (c)	566,000	
Less (a)	-377,000	
Net Assets	189,000	
Available Cash (b) + (d)	72,000	

Interest Rate	Fixed or variable rate	Monthly Repayments €	Annual Repayments €
4.25	Fixed	1500	18,000
18.00		1000	12,000
9.85	Fixed	250	3000
11.00	Fixed	550	6600
10.25	Variable	155	1860
11.00	Variable		
			10,000
			51,460

Interest Rate	Fixed or variable		
0.05%	Variable		
3.50%	Fixed		
?			

Cash Now Value (d)	Loan to Value LTV		
	85%		
	125%		
21,000			
?			
5000			
26,000			

The Available Cash (d) is an estimate of the fire-sale value if you had to sell the assets quickly. Be careful when deciding on the value of investments, as these have fallen significantly. There may also be break costs in withdrawing money from some deposits – tracker deposits and short-term investments – so adjust for these. All values should be on an equal footing, the net realisable value to you after tax, charges and exit or selling costs. Some assets may be unrealisable today because they're locked up until a set maturity date (as is the case with many 'tracker' bonds) or locked up until your retirement age (pension funds).

Preparing a Statement of Affairs

Now that you have completed your financial snapshot you can condense the information to a statement of affairs. You will need this to approach your lenders with your debt repayment proposals.

	Assets (What I Own)	€
	Cash	000
	Deposits (Bank/Building Society/Credit Union)	25,000
	Guaranteed Investments	15,000
	Equity-based Investments	1000
	Cash Value Savings Policies	
A	Total Liquid Assets	41,000
	Pension	120,000
	Investment Properties	250,000
	Business Assets / Net Asset Value	000
	Other Realisable Assets	15,000
B	Total Invested Assets	385,000

	Principal Private Residence (Family Home)	500,000
	Other Personal Assets	15,000
C	Total Assets	900,000

	Liabilities (What I Owe)	€
	Bank Overdraft	5000
	Credit Cards	12,000
	Short Term Debt (1-10 years)	47,000
	Long Term Debt (10 years+)	250,000
	Home Mortgage	350,000
D	Total Liabilities	664,000

E	Net Worth (C-D)	236,000

Note: Under Liquid Assets, include funds that you can quickly cash in or redeem. Some medium-term investments guarantee capital but if you cash them in early they will be worth less. Include this encashment value under Liquid Assets and the difference between this and the guaranteed maturity value under Invested Assets.

Preparing a Minimum Spending Budget

No it was never going to be exciting, but you will be stunned at just how effective monitoring your spending can be and how much stress can be replaced by the feeling of being in control once again. You will be amazed at just how painless it is to save money. It's all pretty quick once you get into the habit, it doesn't lead to catastrophic changes in the quality of your life and it won't leave you feeling like a skinflint – just balanced and informed.

You will find a straightforward template for your spending budget in Appendix 1 but you could just as easily use a jotter and pen or a spreadsheet on a computer, whatever works for you. The important thing is to capture everything you spend and cut out optional spending entirely.

Every Euro you save with good new spending habits is one Euro less borrowed at your highest cost of borrowing. When you're overspending your lifestyle debt is rising so the next Euro you spend isn't yours, it's borrowed, and in most cases that means at credit-card rates of up to 18%.

Be ruthless. You have to get to the absolute bottom line on what you can live on. Go through your expenses five times, asking yourself the question: why this much? You will find ways of cutting lifestyle costs to the bone. You will also unearth expenses you have forgotten about. Once you know what you need to live on, the balance between this figure and what you earn is all you can afford to repay.

Next consider your earnings. Are there any other ways of earning some cash on the side doing odd jobs, giving grinds or tutorials, overseeing exams, driving a taxi part-time? Do you have any tax refunds due? Have you checked that you have claimed all your allowances?

By the end of this exercise you should know three things:

1. How much of a cash lump sum you can get together (if any).
2. How much you will need to live on as a minimum.
3. How much you can afford to repay every month and how sustainable this is.

You have worked out your absolute bottom-line repayment capacity and are now ready for the final step, deciding who is going to get what.

Matching Your Repayment Capacity to Your Debt

This third step will establish the hard facts for the lender. Take this example:

Loan/Debt	Monthly Repayment €	What I Can Afford €	Arrears €	Lump sum Available €	Action
Mortgage	1200	600	3500	None	Interest only
ESB	200	200	500		Pay bill and clear arrears in twelve months
Telephone	120	120	250		Pay bill and clear arrears in twelve months
Heat	100	100			
Car Loan	650	150	1200		Interest only
Credit Card	154	50	1000		Offer €50 per month
Store Card	300	50	1000		Offer €50 per month
Total	2724	1270	7450		

Having gone through the snapshot of their affairs and their spending budget, Martin and Sharon O'Mahoney have calculated that the most they can afford to repay every

month is €1370. They don't have a monthly heating bill but
they pay €1200 a year for home heating that they will have
to allow for monthly. They haven't any savings – nor can
they put together a lump sum to pay off arrears or use
to negotiate a settlement. They decided to make small
payments on their credit cards (which they have already
cut up) to prevent the credit-card providers from chasing
them.

Another example is that of Brendan and Lucy Murphy:

Loan/Debt	Monthly Repayment €	What We Can Afford €	Arrears €	Lump sum Available €	Action
Mortgage	1200	600	3500	1500	Interest only and clear part of arrears
ESB	200	200	500	500	Pay bill and clear arrears
Telephone	120	120	250	250	Pay bill and clear arrears
Heat	100	100			
Car Loan	650	150	1200	250	Interest only
Credit Card	154	50	1000		Offer €50 per month
Store Card	300	50	1000		Offer €50 per month
Total	2724	1270	7450	2500	

The Murphys are in the same boat as the O'Mahoneys except that they have a small lump sum they can use, having sold one of their cars. They have decided that it's best to clear arrears off their priority loans and bills.

Alternative Debt-Settlement Proposals

In some cases it may be possible for you to propose loan settlements to some of your most expensive lenders and clear down your debts with them. Below are examples of workout proposals that you can adapt to fit your position. In practice proposals leading to loan write-offs will vary and will be unique to your personal circumstances. In each of the cases overleaf the loans are distressed: significant arrears have built up. Each couple has gone through most of the steps outlined earlier, arriving at sums they can afford to repay.

John and Mary Neff

What We Can Pay	€
Monthly	900
Lump sum	9,000

What We Owe	To Whom	Balance Owing €	Monthly payment €	Arrears €	Lump Sum €	New Monthly Payment €
Mortgage	Any Bank	300,000	1500	6000	2000	500
Electricity	ESB	600	200	600	600	200
Heating	Local Oil	600	200	600	600	200
Car Loan	GT Finance	25,000	550	1650	1000	Write-off
Credit Card	AAA	10,000		10,000	1500	Write-off
Credit Card	BBB	10,000		10,000	1500	Write-off
Credit Union		10,000	155	620	1300	Write-off
Total		356,200	2605	29,470	8500	900

In this case the Neffs reached an agreement with all the lenders that they would accept lump sum payments and write off the outstanding balance. The car-finance agreement involves handing the car back with a lump sum of €1000 as the car is valued at only €8000. The mortgage lender has agreed to €500 a month, which wouldn't cover the interest on the loan, and to suspend interest for three years. The Neffs' earnings may have improved by then.

Philip and Anne Smith

What We Can Pay	€
Monthly	2100
Lump sum	Nil

What We Owe	To Whom	Balance Owing €	Monthly Payment €	Arrears €	Lump Sum €	New Monthly Payment €
Mortgage	New Bank	300,000	1500	6000		1700
Electricity	ESB	600	200	1000	1000	200
Heating	Lo-Oil	600	200	1000	1000	200
Car Loan	FGR	35,000	800	1650	15,000	
Credit Card	CCC	20,000		10,000	10,000	
Credit Card	BBB	10,000		10,000	5000	
Investment Loan	DKY Co	350,000	1500	8500		
Total		716,200	4200	38,150	32,000	2100

Here the Smiths negotiated a debt-consolidation loan with their mortgage lender and lump sum settlements with others. Their property investment loan is to be cleared once the property has been sold.

Determining Your Revolving Hardcore Debt

Revolving debt never gets paid off in full, it recycles. You process your money through a credit machine that extracts interest and fees on the way through. The balance of these accounts should go to zero, then increase again. Typical

examples are credit-card debt and bank overdrafts that
fluctuate depending on use.

For now just put the current balance and interest rate
down. You will need to work out the hardcore element later.
That's the bit that never gets repaid but remains stuck. Have
a look through your current-account, credit-card and store-
card statements. Is there a level they never go below? Is this
balance increasing balance over time? What you are looking
at is credit that has hardened, which is why it's called
hardcore. The way to deal with this stuff is either to pay it
off or to restructure it into a loan so that it can eventually be
paid off. Once you restructure hardcore into a loan you have
to control your spending.

Look at your current-account statements over the past
number of months. Find the highest balance and lowest
balance and fill out the format below:

Sample of Hardcore Overdraft Analysis

	Month	Month	Month	Month	Month	Month
Limit	-6000	-6000	-6000	-6000	-6000	-6000
Highest Balance	450	-500	-1000	-1500	-3000	-4000
Lowest Balance	-2500	-3000	-3500	-4000	-5000	-6000

You will see in the example that the highest balance has
declined from €450 credit to €4000 overdrawn. At the
same time the lowest balance has declined from €2500
overdrawn to €6000 overdrawn. While the account had an
available overdraft limit of €6000 in the first month, by the

last month there was only €2000 available. This account has a hardcore overdraft of €4000 and climbing.

If you have run out of limit or are banging up against it earlier each month you probably have a hardcore debt problem. You either clear it from savings or refinance it as a loan. Leaving it as it is isn't an option because some day soon your bank will start bouncing cheques and returning loan direct debits. Actions like this always trigger other lenders to take fright and, like a flock of buzzards, take to the skies to track you down. Ideally you shouldn't use any overdraft but if you must, limit it to no more than a quarter of your monthly net income.

If you clear your credit-card balance every month do not put a figure into the repayment column as you are using the card as a transaction card and not a credit card. If you occasionally have a balance running from one month into the next but clear it again, do not put a figure down for repayments. Unless you clear your credit card debt every month you will have balances for which you need to factor in a monthly repayment. Some people pay only the minimum balance requested and others have a figure they pay down every month. Whether you pay the minimum requested or another figure, include it in your calculations as a repayment of debt owing.

Now consider how long it will take you to pay off the balance if you are making the minimum repayment. If you pay the minimum amount of 2.5% of the balance every month it will take you about five years to clear the balance at 18% interest, even if you never used the account again. Remember credit-card interest rates are very high when compared to other debt.

Finding the hardcore on your credit card is easy. It's the bit you haven't repaid. If all you do is lodge a bit when you get your bill and use it up before you get your next bill, the entire balance is hardcore. You are paying nothing off the debt, simply paying interest.

Selling Liquid Assets

These include cash, deposits savings, insurance funds, post office certificates, credit union accounts and anything you think you can sell to realise cash in a reasonable time. If you list a car, boat or a painting, be reasonable as these may have only fire-sale value and not be worth what you think they should be worth. Assets that can be liquidated include paintings, jewellery, collectibles, memorabilia, surplus furniture and antiques – anything you own that you believe you could sell quickly for cash.

Property

Here you should include your family home and other owned properties. Don't include a rented premises unless there is value in the lease you hold. If you own property with someone else, include your share. Be reasonable in your estimates and don't inflate the value to make you feel good. If your house has declined in value by 30%, put down its value today and not what you paid for it. For the latest values go online and check one or two of the property portals for houses in your area.

Cars

Check the used car market and put down the current value and not what you think your car should be worth. Car sales, internet sites and the local paper are indicators of what a car would fetch today, but reduce the price by 10% as car sales prices are always inflated.

Investments
Unless you have a guaranteed maturity value in an investment bond, you are probably below the waterline in value. Most financial assets lost value in 2008 and will take some time to recover. Again, be reasonable and put down the value of the investment today and not what you have invested or what you think it should be worth. If it has a guaranteed maturity date put this value down but remember that cashing in a bond before its guaranteed maturity date may result in substantial losses.

Net Equity
In this column, work out the difference between what you own and what you owe on property and cars. Net equity is an important indicator of your capacity to raise additional finance and also an indicator of which loans you should pay down fast.

LTV (Loan to Value)
This ratio, which expresses your loan as a percentage of the house value, is a key risk measure for your mortgage lenders. If LTV is above 100% it means you are in negative-equity land. Below it and you may be doing OK. It depends on how much below the line you are and how you are managing your repayments. If you get into arrears problems your lender will be very conscious of the LTV, as this can worsen quite dramatically over a very short period of time.

10

The Inside Story of Debt Recovery

These are unprecedented times. Borrowers are experiencing a level of distressed debt and debt default unimaginable during the halcyon days of the boom. Lenders are beginning to recognise the degree of their own responsibility in aggressively flogging debt to anyone who wanted money. They are nervously monitoring the growing number of mortgage holders one, two and three months in arrears, knowing full well that it is the tip of the iceberg, that their unsecured loan book will get worse.

Here's the biggest secret in banking, the stuff you will never hear a bank openly admit: the cost of recovering debt defaults can absorb up to half of moneys recovered – so banks prefer cheaper and softer options like rescheduling repayments and, if necessary, writing off part of the debt owed when they believe a reliable customer can commit to servicing the remainder. But don't expect this treatment from banks who calculate that their assets are at high risk whether from other faster-moving debt recovery agencies, fecklessness or bad sub-prime borrowers. In these circum-stances banks, especially sub-prime lenders, will bare their teeth and vigorously pursue defaulters through the courts. Such lenders risk unfavourable judgements if borrowers can establish that debt was mis-sold to them but can rely on the courts where it's clear that borrowers have failed to face up to their position.

Although there will always be a hard core number of reckless borrowers used to abusing credit markets, most distressed debtors in this cycle will emerge from ordinary middle Ireland, totally at sea with distressed debt and unused to how the system works.

On the face of it, Jill McGrath was doing well. She drove a flash 08 Mercedes, wore designer clothes and owned an up-market pad across from O2. Like her friends she worked hard and thoroughly enjoyed her time off, socialising and shopping. But under the surface of Jill's lifestyle lay a ticking time-bomb. Jill had a lifestyle that many would envy, but it was all built on credit and her borrowings increased as a result of her lavish spending in the two years leading to the credit crunch and recession. Today Jill has a mortgage of €350,000 that she topped up with a no-questions-asked credit union loan of €30,000 to furnish the pad. Her Merc is financed on a lease of €35,000 which she topped up, borrowing the down payment from one of her three credit cards.

One of Jill's credit card has a balance of €10,000 and the others €7500 each, not counting her store card with an up-market clothing retailer. Her bank overdraft is €5000 and is constantly at its limit as her salary disappears in loan repayments the minute it arrives in her account. In fact Jill has been living on her credit cards for nearly two years. Last month Jill's boss announced a sharp drop in sales and an 80% cut in bonuses this year. Jill had counted on the cash to meet the increasing demands of her lenders, as she's been slipping into arrears. While Jill still has a job, her income is about to halve.

In all Jill owes money to six different lenders and her credit rating with the Irish Credit Bureau is about to change from a healthy green to a glaring shade of red. Jill has a dilemma – she owes more than €445,000 but hasn't the income to make the repayments and is about to meet the unfriendly faces of at least six lenders, all of whom want to be repaid first.

Clearly there's a need for Jill to get a grip on her finances. And there's also a need for her lenders to get a grip on a new reality: that Jill does not have the means to pay off her loans for the foreseeable future. It's not that Jill doesn't want to. She is an honourable person, shattered by the consequences of her excesses. She regrets not moderating her lifestyle after she bought the apartment, but money was easy and her friends kept whisking her out to parties and shops just as before. Now, even with the best will in the world, Jill simply cannot generate the cash to pay off the loans. So what will happen?

Jill will continue to get demanding letters and phone calls from lenders. She will hear at length from aggressive and typically young and poorly-trained collection agents who couldn't care less about her as a person and whose employers are interested only in grabbing the largest possible slice of her income. Jill will eventually get down to doing her budget and figure out what she can afford to pay and to which lender. She may seek professional help to prepare the ground for negotiation but the current old-fashioned legal system for debt-collection may mean that she will experience the trauma and stigma of court appearances extending over two to three years. Ideally she needs a plan.

The good news is that this guide can help Jill to plan her way out of the mire of distressed debt.

But how will lenders react to a proactive debt settlement approach? In some other countries Jill could enter into a common arrangement with her creditors. She could use the services of a debt counsellor who would draw up a plan, setting out her means and what she can afford to repay in total every month. Then her creditors would agree to accept a share of this in full settlement of her loans. This means that Jill would have to repay, say, half the lifestyle debt she owes over five years. At the end of the five-year period she would be clear of her debts.

Jill's mortgage finance falls into a different category but it would be included in these arrangements if negative equity were involved. Once the creditors 'voted' to accept the arrangement the deal would be done and would be overseen by the facilitator. It would be for all intents and purposes a binding agreement that would clear Jill's debts over time if she stuck to it. These types of schemes operate in countries such as the UK and Canada and elsewhere in Europe. But what about Ireland? There are no such structures in Ireland but it is possible to engineer similar outcomes. It takes strong and honest presentation and lots of hard graft to get all the horses to water but the pressing circumstances of the current market may propel more lenders into these types of arrangements.

Never Snub Your Lender

When borrowers run into cashflow difficulties and default on repayments they often make the mistake of ignoring communications from their lenders. This is the worst thing you can do. Your silence guarantees that the crisis loan will now escalate within the strict procedures established by lenders to deal with defaulters. If the lender fails to reach you or come to some agreement about repayments this will inevitably result in your file being handed to their solicitors or a debt-collection agency. The latter can make life miserable with constant harsh reminders to pay up or face a court judgement. Such a judgement could result in a visit by a sheriff appointed by the court to confiscate goods to the value of the outstanding debt. In addition, surcharge interest can be added to the outstanding balance, making the problem greater than ever.

Lenders expect a certain percentage of borrowers to run into difficulties and have established procedures to work through the difficulty with the customer. Most lenders will agree to lower repayments temporarily but won't agree to anything if you just block them off.

> You cannot pay what you cannot afford no matter how insistent or pressurising any lender is.

How the Process of Debt-Recovery Works

Before you read this section you need to understand one thing. Once you borrow money it becomes legally yours, not the bank's. When you entered your loan agreement you promised to repay a debt from income you would subsequently earn. If circumstances force you to break that promise the bank has the legal right to demand that you make your repayments or pay off the entire amount owing. If you fail to make repayments after they have demanded that you do so, you breach your contract and the bank can formally escalate matters. Only when you have failed to repay on its formal demand can it rely on any security or collateral you may have given. Your house is legally yours and not the bank's. Your car is legally yours and not the bank's unless you have a lease.

If you believe that you will soon find yourself in financial trouble and have problems making your loan repayments the first thing you should do is tell your lenders. This gives them advance notice and establishes a clear indication of your honesty and proactiveness. Should you end up in court, you can point to the fact that you informed your lenders at the earliest possible stage. See Appendix 5 for a specimen letter to use at this stage.

The fateful day arrives and you are at the point where you cannot make repayments. You write again, tell your lender about your problems and look for an early meeting to discuss things. (Meanwhile you have followed the steps outlined earlier in the book to establish exactly how much you can afford to repay and to whom.) See Appendix 5 for a specimen letter you can use at this stage.

Lenders will be trying to get the arrears paid in full and some may not to want to hear about your problems. Your experience could vary greatly, depending on the company and the employee involved. How the opening, more informal, stage is handled is largely down to the lender.

Credit unions have a well-earned and enviable reputation for their flexible and understanding approach to debt. In the main, banks also take a personal approach and will agree to discuss people's debt problems face-to-face.

There are two distinct debt-collection approaches used by lenders, depending on your loan: one applies to mortgage arrears and repossessions, the other to unsecured debt arrears.

If you have a mortgage the lender has the right to seek an order for repossession and sell your home or property. You agreed to this action when you signed your mortgage deed, which is a legal document. Of course a bank is entitled to recover only what it is owed plus its costs and will have to pay you whatever is left.

Banks and credit unions stress one important message: if you anticipate having a problem making loan repayments, contact your lenders immediately to tell them.

If the lender has no security it must go through quite a lengthy legal process to prove the debt and seek court sanction for various debt-collection processes. Typical unsecured loans include credit card, hire purchase, credit-union loans and bank term loans.

If you have a mortgage and an unsecured loan with the same bank, the bank must go through the unsecured loan process. The bank cannot rely on the mortgage for both types of loan unless you originally agreed it could. If you have a mix of mortgage and unsecured loans from the same lender you should carefully study your loan agreements and get advice on your legal position.

Contrary to popular opinion, most cases of borrowers defaulting on mortgages don't end up in court with lenders looking for possession orders. Instead, home-owners, having exhausted all other possibilities and burned through their savings to meet monthly mortgage payments, eventually raise the white flag after arrears build up and surrender their homes directly to the bank.

Your mortgage agreement will list the powers of the bank when you go into arrears, so ask for a copy of your mortgage deed from the solicitor who acted for you on the purchase. Before you hand over the keys of your house to a lender get advice, as you could remain liable for substantial costs before your house is sold off. Voluntary handovers are not as clean-cut as they would appear.

No data is available about this trend but with most large lenders experiencing several thousand home-owners in arrears it's safe to say that numbers of handovers are increasing. Much like banks in Germany during the post-reunification slump, Irish banks are set to become the biggest landlords in the country, renting out houses and awaiting price recovery just like everyone else! Banks are on the horns of a dilemma. Understanding that dilemma is the key to your renegotiation position.

Most distressed debt will be among borrowers who bought at inflated prices and whose properties are worth less than the debt – that is, borrowers with negative equity. It stands to reason that banks, in these circumstances, don't want the house back on their books if they can possibly avoid it.

Going after repossessions through the courts and holding property is very costly: not only do banks end up with an asset they can't sell in the current market except at a giveaway price and a recognised bad debt on their books, they'll have a fat legal bill. Get the picture? Banks want to settle: they don't want to go to court and risk damage to their reputation that could impact on new mortgage sales.

To take advantage of this you will have to be honest and get moving at an early stage. If you haven't done your snapshot and budget, do them now. Write to your mortgage lender. Tell them you will miss repayments and why.

11

Mortgage Arrears
and Repossession

Because of our history, home repossession is a very emotive subject in Ireland. Commentators have written about the dilemma people face when they have defaulted on their mortgages and are faced with losing their homes as lenders seek court orders for repossession. But fears of an explosion in repossessions may yet prove misplaced. The gigantic property slump is new territory for Irish banks, whose own share prices have been decimated because of fears about mounting bad debts as a result of sloppy property and development lending. The recession, the dramatic collapse in house prices and the near-stagnant house market have caused everyone to mark time. The possible full nationalisation of all the Irish banks may change matters further.

The housing situation is unprecedented, with almost 70,000 housing units on the market. Another measure of the inflated nature of the bubble are the 470,000 planning permissions that were granted over the last few years. The countryside is dotted with silent half-built sites sprouting weeds, not homes. Other developments are finished but eerily silent witnesses to the property implosion. 'See-through' office blocks are empty of tenants and vacant retail outlets carry the names of auctioneers who are laying off staff and fighting for survival. Within a year the construction industry, once the engine of growth, ground to a halt. Tens of thousands of workers have been laid off and dozens of building firms have gone bust. The papers that once proudly sponsored the booming property market with commentators forecasting a soft landing are now struggling as revenue from advertising property dries up.

Nowhere else has the property bust been felt as acutely as in Ireland, which has one of the highest home-ownership rates on the planet on the planet. Borrowers now owe lenders more than €35bn in property loans and €140bn in home mortgages. At the time of writing, house prices had fallen by 20% on average from peak prices in late 2006, with predictions that they would drop by at least 50%. In 2007 the value of housing stock was €516bn. If house prices fall by 50% this means that house owners will have lost €198bn in household wealth.

There are currently about 350,000 vacant homes in Ireland. The figures include 60,000 unoccupied holiday homes and a whopping 255,000 unrented houses. About 17% of Irish houses are unoccupied. Ireland has about 300,000 rented home units in all, which means that the country currently has more unrented than rented units when holiday homes are counted. There are many property investors desperate to get out of the worst investments they've ever made. Those who invested in houses at peak prices using interest-only loans and who are now facing capital repayments are being squeezed into selling at any price. It's hard to see how there can be any hope for an increase in house prices until all this excess inventory is cleared, something that will take several years.

If Irish mortgage lenders are to be believed the rate of repossessions has increased slightly but it is nothing like the experience of countries that have a more ruthless approach such as the UK and US. The statistics tend to back up this claim. Bankers say there is a different cultural attitude to repossessions in Ireland but they *would* say that. There are no figures available for jingle mail, the number of people who have voluntarily surrendered their homes, putting the keys in the post to the lender.

The Financial Regulator requires mortgage lenders to write to you immediately and inform you that you have missed a payment. Most were doing this anyway but some were a tad slow. This doesn't mean you shouldn't be first past the post and tell your lender about your problem *before* you miss your repayment! Otherwise you can expect to get a letter telling you about the missed repayment and requesting you to make immediate payment or contact the lender if you cannot. If you haven't told your mortgage lender about your financial difficulties, now is the time to do so.

The vast majority of people will give priority to paying their mortgage so bankers know that if a mortgage loan goes into arrears, the chances are that other loans are already in arrears. You can save everyone's time by telling them the truth about your financial situation.

Depending on your situation you have a number of options at this time:

- A repayment holiday: your monthly repayments are rolled up and added to your loan for a period unlikely to exceed six months. The objective is to give you breathing space to get back on your feet – for instance until you find a new job – but when repayments recommence the debt will be higher and so will be the monthly repayments.

- A switch from making capital repayments to making interest payments only for a period of time. Depending on the strength of your position this could be agreed for a period of several years. The benefit to cashflow could be quite considerable: for example, repayments on a twenty-year mortgage of €500,000 costing a little over €3,000 per month would fall to just €1,667 per month at a fixed interest rate of 4%. Interest-only mortgages are highly sensitive to rising interest rates so, if it's available, a fixed rate makes sense in these very uncertain times.
- An extension of the mortgage term can also help to ease the burden on your monthly cashflow if you have a reasonably short mortgage term. For example if you extend a fifteen-year investment mortgage to thirty years, the monthly repayments will reduce by about one third. However this extension will double the total interest you will have paid the bank by the time the debt is cleared
- A debt-consolidation loan whereby you consolidate all your loans into your mortgage. By doing so you can reduce the monthly cost of repayments but at the cost of paying a far higher amount of interest in the long term.

You can expect to get another letter if you miss a second mortgage repayment. If your lender is on the ball they will already have tried to make direct contact with you, usually by phone. Talking is better than writing. Lenders know that the earlier they make contact the better it is for both parties.

If you miss a third repayment the next letter will be quite stern and tell you that you must bring your arrears up to date. Your lenders will demand a meeting to discuss your arrears and threaten to pass your account to a debt-collection agency if you don't pay.

This is the first step to legal debt recovery. You are now on the road to repossession. By this time the vast majority of loan workouts have been agreed. That is, if you have been talking and not running away.

Your home remains yours even if the outstanding mortgage is more than the value of your house. The lender has to take a few further steps. The first thing they will do is to call in the loan in full. This means you must now repay the full amount owing, and failing this the lender will seek a court order for possession, citing your arrears as cause for their action. You still have time – it is quite common for agreements to be reached right up to the day of the court hearing.

Even if a bank gets a possession order on your home it may not exercise it but may instead seek an agreement from the strong position in which it finds itself. Alternatively, the judge may stay the order providing that you bring your arrears up to date or reach an agreement on a workout with the lender. At this late stage you may still rescue the situation.

Sub-Prime Lenders

These lenders offered mortgages with higher interest rates to Irish borrowers who had been refused loans by the main retail banks and tended to adopt a harsher policy when arrears occurred, rapidly escalating the collection process and moving for repossession in the courts. One sub-prime lender, Smart Mortgages, frequently popped up in court reports with applications for possession orders, most of which were successful, although – as has become increasingly common – the judge in the case reported below granted a stay on possession, forcing the lender to consider other options:

> A family whose small business was hit hard by the slump in new-house construction had arranged a mortgage with Smart Mortgages as revenues dried up. The repossession case was heard in 2008. Arrears of €18,500 had accumulated, mounting at a rate of €1000 per month. The judge granted Smart Mortgages possession but gave a stay for six months to allow the family to repay the full moneys outstanding to the lender, failing which the lender would take full possession. In this case the family explained that it had some land adjacent to the house that it hoped to sell to meet the debt.

Sub-prime lenders in Ireland are obliged to comply with the Financial Regulator's Consumer Protection Code. The loophole in Irish law that allowed some of these lenders to remain unregulated was closed in 2008. This means that the Regulator can now mandate sub-prime lenders to adopt the new code on mortgage arrears, introduced as part of the government's banking recapitalisation programme (as described below).

The Government's Response to Mortgage Arrears

As the shocking reality of joblessness became clear through-out late 2008 and early 2009, the banks maintained that their mortgage arrears were not too bad. However, the inevitable consequence of so many people losing their jobs, with many Irish businesses failing, and a steep drop in real income for nearly everyone else, is that mortgage arrears will dramatically escalate and probably spike alarmingly by late 2009. The Irish government, concerned that many homes might be repossessed, has taken its lead from the Irish Bankers' Federation (IBF) voluntary code of practice on mortgage arrears (see below). IBF members – the main banks and mortgage lenders – have been using the code since 2000. But as with all voluntary codes, some members observe it better than others.

As part of its programme to recapitalise the banks, the government proposes to transform the IBF voluntary code into a mandatory code, subject to regulatory scrutiny and penalties for non-compliance. The new code applies to all mortgage lenders including sub-prime operations. In a separate initiative, the government will also amend the laws that allow a mortgage lender to repossess a home. In future, it seems that a lender will have to apply to repossess and show cause. The fact that repayments have not been made will not automatically permit the lender to repossess.

As I write, Bank of Ireland and AIB have agreed to delay starting repossession proceedings for twelve months under the government's recapitalisation programme. Other lenders are likely to follow suit as the Financial Regulator adopts the IBF voluntary code on mortgage arrears as a mandatory code.

Recently, the judiciary has been taking a dim view of the aggressive home-repossession tactics of some lenders and denied or 'stayed' (delayed) orders for possession, roundly condemning the lenders for reckless lending. The Master of the High Court has said that repossession will not be permitted as a matter of course as in a recession of historic proportions many, if not most, borrowers are not to blame for their arrears and no one gains from rows of empty, shuttered houses.

Lenders will have to refer people to debt counselling as part of the arrears process. Organisations such as MABS must be provided with the funding and resources required if they are to respond effectively to this national mortgage crisis and help to implement this initiative.

The Irish Bankers' Federation (IBF) Voluntary Code on Mortgage Arrears

Under the IBF code, lenders agree to adopt flexible procedures for the handling of arrears cases and to assist borrowers as far as possible. Lenders will not seek repossession of the property until every reasonable effort has been made to agree an alternative repayment schedule. The following are among the key features of the IBF code:

- a commitment to handle genuine cases sympathetically and positively
- a willingness to explore, on a case-by-case basis, the suitability of various options, including changing the amount of the regular repayment, temporary deferral of the repayments, extending the term of the loan and capitalising the arrears and interest.
- You can download a copy of the code at www.ibf.ie or read a summary in Appendix 7.

12

Unsecured Debt Arrears and the Legal Process

Some lenders use mechanised systems to pursue borrowers, employing junior staff members who go through the motions, working off a script. This happens mainly with unsecured debts such as credit cards. One credit-card provider has a habit of phoning borrowers a number of times a day, which is annoying if you haven't any money to pay them. Legally you are entitled to protection from harassment at work or outside working hours under the Consumer Credit Act and can report any breaches to the Director of Consumer Protection at IFSRA, the Financial Regulator, who is mandated to investigate and take action.

(Practitioners privately say that many people are better off waiting until the debt-handling is switched from this type of robotic employee to a collection agency where experts have some sense of human psychology and are not driven by computer systems and the demands of supervisors. Not that either is pleasant…)

Banks are redeploying staff from selling loans into debt recovery so as soon as you miss a month you can expect the treatment to begin. You can expect, at this point, to have your own, specially assigned, loan officer!

Credit finance companies and store-card creditors have well-oiled processes. They religiously make contact day after day. They know they're the last in the pile. Their modus operandi is to get to you first. The better ones ring you before your next repayment is due to remind you to make your repayment. If they are not on your priority list remember to be nice and refer them to the letter you should already have sent them explaining your situation. They will persist. More missed repayments will trigger further letters and calls and the language will begin to harden. By the third letter you will typically be told that debts are being handed over for legal collection. In almost all cases this means that your account is outsourced to a debt-collection agency or a firm of solicitors specialising in legal debt-collection.

You will then get a formal legal letter demanding payment of arrears on your loan and, depending on the type of loan account, full immediate repayment. Depending on the amount you owe, the lender can pursue legal action in the district, circuit or high court. The current limits are: up to €6349.00 in the district court; €6349-€38,092 in the circuit court; and in excess of €38,092 in the high court.

Court is the worse place to settle anything. Matters should be settled by mutual agreement if at all possible. But if you ignore letters and other communications from lenders, they will issue proceedings. If lenders are pursuing you, look for advice. Contact MABS, who provide an excellent free and confidential debt-counselling service. You can also contact your Free Legal Aid centre for advice and in some cases they may arrange representation in court.

There are two things your lender's solicitor needs to do. The first is to prove the debt and the second to obtain a ruling from the judge on this amount. This is called a judgement.

The first thing you will receive is a civil summons, which is an official notice of the claim being made by the lender. You will be told that on a certain date the lender will go to the court to obtain a judgement against you. If it's a circuit-court process this is called a civil bill and if it's the high court it's called a summary summons.

You do not have to appear in court but you can choose to contest the bill or summons. If you do you will need to have your own solicitor to represent you. Most consumer debts are not contested at all. Once the debt has been proven or a defended case heard in court, the court may issue a judgement against you. You will also be liable for costs. These are scaled according to the court in question and are the only costs that can be recovered from you. Once the judgement is issued the interest charged on the arrears you owe is fixed at a rate of 8%. This is the maximum that can be charged by the lender even if the balance of your loan is charged at a higher rate. For example if your arrears on a car loan are €4000 and the balance is €15,000 a maximum rate of 8% is all that can be charged on the €4000 arrears.

The lender has a number of options. They will register the judgement, which allows them to publish it in *Stubbs Gazette* and Experian *All-Ireland Gazette*. This means that the information is made available to the public at large and may be reported on by the media. The lender may also tell any other lender to whom you owe money about your difficulties. The judgement will be recorded by your lender at the Irish Credit Bureau. Judgements against you last for twelve years unless you settle the amount owing. If you do settle, you can apply to have the judgement set aside or 'satisfied'.

Judgement Mortgages

If you have a house or property, including land, the lender can have a judgement mortgage registered against your property. This means that should you ever sell the property or your home you will have to pay off the amount owing on the judgement and any interest owing on the amount.

While the lender can't take possession of your house as when they have a legal mortgage, they can apply to the court for what is called a 'Well Charging Order and Order for Sale' of the property. Whether a lender is allowed to do this depends on the equity you have in your property, the amount you owe other lenders on your mortgage and of course the judge. Most judges will not permit the forced sales of family homes so lenders apply for a judgement mortgage in the hope that some time in the future you will sell the property and be able to repay them. The judgement mortgage is valid for twelve years.

Involving a Sheriff for Execution

Each county in Ireland has a sheriff, who is a civil servant. One of the sheriff's jobs is to seize and sell goods belonging to debtors in discharge of a debt. There can be long delays and a sheriff often decides the debtor has nothing worth seizing and selling.

Instalment Orders

Instalment orders are the preferred choice of most lenders. An instalment order means that the district court can legally instruct you to pay a regular instalment on your loan arrears. You will get a court summons asking you to appear in court, where you will be asked to explain and prove what you owe, earn and spend. This is where all your work on your snapshot and budget comes into play. By now you may have received professional help to prepare your statement of means for the court. But a debt counsellor cannot represent you – only you or your solicitor can do so. The judge will decide what level of weekly/monthly repayments you are to make to the lender. More often than not judges will not give instalment orders against unemployed people or people whose only income is some form of social welfare payment.

If you don't make the repayments the court has ordered you to make you will be in contempt of court. Your lender can go back to the court and seek to have you committed to prison for non-payment. This is called a committal order. In genuine cases of financial hardship a judge will not send someone to prison. But if you are one of the few people who deliberately and knowingly decide not to make your repayments and you have the money to do so, you risk going to prison.

If you are served with a summons, you must appear and be prepared once again to prove that you do not have the means to make the payments. A judge may reduce the instalment amount to a level you can afford.

Such is our outdated debt-collection system that you could end up facing multiple court appearances as each individual lender pursues you in court. Currently there is nothing you can do to prevent this from happening.

The court may order a person who owes money to the defaulter to pay it directly to the lender in a 'garnishee' order. This usually involves large sums and high-court cases. For example a farmer may be due a grant from government. If the bank knows this they can look to garnishee the grant and the government will pay the amount to the bank. A similar order is used if you owe money for tax. The Revenue can acquire an attachment order forcing someone who owes money to a defaulter to pay this money directly to Revenue.

Personal Bankruptcy

Filing for personal bankruptcy is the nuclear option. If you become bankrupt your creditors can no longer pursue you in court. Everything you own will be sold off to pay your debts and you will have to make payments to a legally-appointed person whose job is to liquidate your assets and pay off your creditors.

A lender can have you declared a bankrupt in the high court if you fail to pay debts on foot of a judgement – typically if you fail to pay an instalment order and after a sheriff declares you have no goods to sell. Your debt must be more than €1905.00. In practice bankruptcy is a lengthy and expensive process. It is far more common in other countries, including Britain, than it is in Ireland, where the costs, restrictions and time involved make it a less-favoured route to seeking protection from mounting creditor pressure.

The debtor makes a declaration of bankruptcy, passing control of his or her financial affairs and all assets to a trustee who deals with all the creditors as well as possible from the remaining assets. Once the process is complete, the court lifts restrictions on the bankrupt person from doing business and they can start over, with a credit record in the gutter and usually with nothing left.

A more common approach and the one I advocate is a voluntary contractual settlement with all creditors. The debtor assembles a reasonable and honest proposal and enters into negotiation, agreement is reached and the debts discharged. In the absence of a formal framework, depending on their financial skills and the complexities of the situation, the debtor will probably need professional help.

Business Debts

Lots of Irish people who will end up with distressed debt also run a business and are therefore trying to coping not just with conventional retail banks pressing in on mortgage arrears but with a host of business-related creditors, all seeking settlements of accounts. Most small business owners operate as sole traders, a less costly and simpler model than a limited company. However, the advantage of having a limited company is that, unless creditors of an insolvent limited company can establish that it was operated recklessly, the debts of the company can be recovered only from its assets. The claims of creditors do not extend to the personal assets of the owners, unless they have given personal guarantees. Not so for sole traders, whose personal assets are exposed to creditors in the event of a failure to repay debts.

Even directors of limited companies can be exposed, especially for commercial mortgages covered by personal guarantees or mortgages that were effected personally to begin with – usually where their limited companies are the tenants in the properties the directors bought personally with bank finance. A sharp recession can lead to lots of distressed debt as business owners vainly attempt to trade out of it. If businesses don't match the scale of the downturn by cutting costs, debts can mount fast.

When a limited company becomes distressed and negotiations with creditors fail, the owner can make an application to court seeking protection from creditors. If this is granted by the judge it allows breathing space for the owner to assemble a proposal to pay back part of the amounts owing to creditors, usually by the sale of personal assets. The court calls creditors to a meeting to vote on the proposal. The agreement requires a 60% majority, representing at least

60% of the debts outstanding, and is then rubber-stamped by the court.

Things to Look Out For

- Beware of the high-pressure debt-collection tactics of unsecured lenders. Some unsecured lenders strike fast, trying to grab the largest possible slice of your income for themselves. They race to the courts to get a judge to grant an instalment order.

- If you are really unlucky, you could find yourself coming under severe pressure from your least important creditors. It's your job not to allow this to happen. You should have already decided who is going to be repaid and how much they are going to be repaid. If some creditors are left out in the cold, so be it for now. Be clear and firm with them. You intend paying them off once you have the income to do so. If they pursue you through the courts they do so at their own peril. At worst you might expect one or two of them to try to get a judgement and have it registered.

- It's likely that you will get demand letters, usually generated by a computer-tracking system, even where you are negotiating with your lender.

- Focus on getting the agreement of your creditors to your repayment plan, not *their* version of a repayment plan, which could mean that a priority creditor is not repaid.

- Be firm. Remember that you have done your homework. You have prepared your budget and know what you can afford to pay.

- Don't let lenders trawl through your budget. Tell them it's none of their business. You owe them money, nothing else.

- Once you are certain what you can genuinely afford to pay – and I know this is easy to say – you are in quite a strong bargaining position.
- Don't be proud. If you need help contact your local MABS office or Free Legal Aid Centre or hire a professional.

13

Negative Equity

Owen bought his home for €350,000 in 2007, borrowing €315,000 – 90% – from his bank over a term of thirty years. His contribution of €35,000 was his equity in his home. If his home had increased in value by 10% over the first year, his equity would have increased by €35,000, plus the amount repaid off his mortgage capital and less the cost of servicing the interest. This is the positive side of gearing. But property prices have been falling, not rising, since he bought his house.

Two years later Owen owes €310,000 but his house has dropped in value by 20% to €280,000, so he owes more than he owns. Owen owns what the Americans call an upside-down home. His negative equity is €30,000. If he sold today he would lose his hard-saved equity of €35,000 plus another €30,000, having forked out interest of €31,500. In total he'd lose €96,500. In the event of a 50% decline in house value, Owen's upside-down mortgage would translate into a balance-sheet loss in excess of €206,000.

If Owen is to regain lost ground his house, now worth 20% less than he paid for it, will have to increase in value by 25%. However if prices decline by 50% he'll needs another property boom to recover lost ground, as prices would have to double to get him back to his starting value. In the meantime he's paying interest on a debt much larger than his home value.

Owen is in a typical negative-equity trap. He is tied to his house. If he sells it he will have to come up with the difference or pay it off over time. He will be left with no equity to invest in a new home and he will owe €30,000. As long as Owen keeps his job and can afford his loan repayments, his home is not at risk. But his mobility is impaired because he is stuck with this property and its negative equity.

Owen works in Galway and has been offered a job in Dublin. His options are to (a) rent the house and hope the rent will cover the loan repayments or (b) sell the house at a loss and buy another in Dublin if he can find the €30,000 required by his lender to clear the debt. Owen might convince his lender to let him sell and move, adding the negative equity to his new mortgage.

'Negative equity' is one of those headlines the media often use to measure the effect of a property slump as values fall below the mortgages attached to them. In the final few years of the property bubble, lending criteria relaxed, allowing ever more borrowers to finance their homes with little or nothing down. In 2006 alone, 50% of borrowers took up the offer of 100% finance. The subsequent decline in property values, already -30% by the beginning of 2009, created an estimated negative-equity trap of about €14 billion. In the final three years of the bubble 140,000 new mortgages were effected, most of which represented more than 90% of the purchase price of the properties. In many cases the remaining 10% did not come from savings held by borrowers, but from concealed loans from credit unions and relatives.

John and Mary O'Sullivan bought their house for €250,000 in 2006, with a 100% mortgage over twenty-five years. Their mortgage rate is now 3.5%. At this point, they are facing a negative-equity trap because the value of their house has dropped to €187,500 – a fall of 25%. As they owe €236,483 on their loan, their negative equity – the difference between the value of their home and their loan – is €48,983.00. The model below illustrates how the negative equity in their home might decline as property values recover.

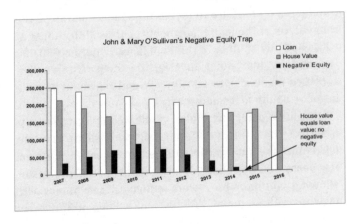

1. The white column represents the mortgage declining as the O'Sullivans make their monthly repayments.
2. The grey column is the value of their home as it declines and then begins to rise.
3. The black column is their negative-equity trap, which at first increases and then declines.

If property prices fall by 45% by 2010, then rise at 5% a year, the combination of declining loan and rising house value will erode the O'Sullivans' negative equity by 2015. Should their home increase in value by 5% a year from 2011 onwards its worth won't reach the €250,000 they paid for it until 2023. The illustration uses current predictions on medium-term interest rates and predicted falls in house price. Of course, interest rates may rise and fall and property may not decline as much and may recover more quickly than this illustration suggests. But it may be wishful thinking to predict anything less than a prolonged stagnation in property prices. If they can keep their jobs, John and Mary may yet be bailed out by a prolonged period of high inflation which will erode the real value of the outstanding debt while pushing up property prices in nominal terms. But this is by no means certain.

Negative equity won't sink you provided you can wait for many years for the next strong up-cycle and continue to meet repayments. In the meantime it may, however, impinge on your ability to raise substantial credit elsewhere, especially if lenders see a negative balance sheet. It's a particularly nasty trap if you cannot afford repayments and you're forced to sell or your home is repossessed – you will still owe the balance. In this scenario, having lost your home, you clearly have no means of repaying the balance and the likelihood is that the lender will write it off.

The Car Trap

Few of us ever consider the negative equity trap in cars. We roll over loans in ever-increasing amounts and never build up equity. It's only when the crunch comes, repayments are a burden and used-car values plummet that the car trap crystallises.

> Susan, a middle-aged businesswoman, bought her dream car, a brand-new luxury four-litre SUV, for €60,000 in January 2008. At that time, using the 'R' word was frowned upon

and Susan bought into the Ahern government guff about a soft landing, pointing to that government's unblemished economic record. After getting €10,000 on her trade-in, she borrowed €50,000 from her bank, a loan that is costing her €800 monthly in repayments.

A year later, Susan owes €44,500 to the bank and business conditions have really tightened. Meanwhile the used car market has been flooded with luxury SUVs. Today Susan's car is worth €35,000 at an auction – that's if she's lucky. Her negative equity is already €9500 and she's lost the €10,000 she added to the deal plus the €4200 in interest she's already paid. When she sells the vehicle her total loss is €23,700. Susan ends up selling the SUV and buying an older car but she owes the bank €9,500 on a vehicle she no longer owns. Susan is thinking of voting for some other party next time around.

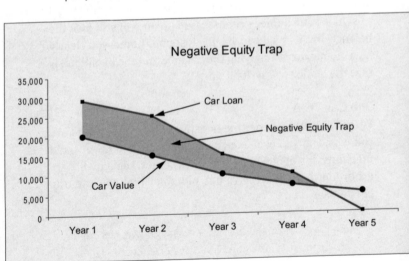

If you do borrow to buy a car remember that the car depreciates faster than your loan. Take out three-year loans if possible and try to build some equity if you want to trade in the car in three years' time.

The graph plots the falling value of a car against the outstanding loan. The car, which cost €30,000, was financed by a loan of €30,000. The values decline at different rates but for almost the entire five years of the loan the borrower has negative equity in the car, owing more than the vehicle is worth.

14

Some Cost-Control Tips
for the Recession

The Department of Finance sets a target for cutbacks, then goes about finding places to cut – not the other way around. So should you! Resolve to cut 20% of all costs within three months and then figure out how to do it. When you have done so, reward yourself! Here are a few pointers for saving money on lifestyle spending:

- Mistakes are common, so always check your bills.
- Write up a list for your weekly household shop and stick to it to avoid impulse-buying. Always shop for high-price items like a new coat or shoes with a preset budget.
- Never shop when you're starving or you will stuff your trolley and your mouth as you shop like there's going to be a meteor strike.
- Check your weekly household shop for unnecessary spending on silly things like premium-brand dog food, bottled water and fizzy drinks. The dog might like the change to cheaper own brands, a filter jug is probably just as effective as bottled water and what about giving the kids sugar-free dilutable drinks instead?
- Ignore supermarket loyalty cards which are designed to lure you into the one shop all the time. Switch to discount stores like Lidl and Aldi for your weekly basics and top up at elsewhere for the remainder. Keep an eagle eye out

for bargains like reduced price, promotions, half-price and buy one get one free campaigns. New competition arriving is great for price wars so watch out for ways to save money by switching telecom companies, gyms and insurers.

- Lunches and lattes are bad for the girth and lousy on the pocket. If you spend €10 a day on lunch food that's about €2200 in a working year. Why not make your own lunch and bring it to work? The latte habit will cost another €1000 or so a year. Make your own or be real cool and switch to green tea. Get Barrys!
- Buy clothes that last and wait for the sales. Some outlets sell stock at fantastic discounts, frequently more than 50%. Separate buying clothes that are needed from forking out a bundle on designer gear that looks good but quickly goes out of fashion.
- Make www.consumerconnect.ie one your favourites on the computer. It's the National Consumer Association website, chock-full of money saving ideas and value-for-money surveys.
- Share money-saving ideas with your friends, keep in touch with good consumer journalism and stay vigilant for new opportunities to cut costs as price discounting begins in earnest in recessionary Ireland, the opposite of the boom activity of lashing on fat margins.

Ask for the Recession Discount!

Here's the hottest tip – ask for discounts on just about all goods and services in the private sector and you're likely to get between 10% and 35% off pre-recession prices. The scale of inflated profit margins in many sectors is becoming clear. This confirms earlier calculations by the Consumer

Strategy Group (forerunner of the NCA) that, after allowing for Ireland's higher-input costs and lower corporation tax, Irish prices seemed about one quarter inflated when compared to Europe – and that's allowing for normal profit. That's the Rip-Off Republic margin that was tolerated by widespread consumer inertia. So expect a minimum 25% off all goods and services: builders, architects, solicitors, cars, kitchens, white goods – you name it. Just insist, then close your mouth and wait in silence for the reply!

Cut Your Telephone Charges

Whether fixed or mobile, this is a major cost item for an average family that can amount to more than €3000 a year. How many times have you received a bill, only to choke on your cornflakes because your charges have gone through the roof? When you read the spreadsheet that lists your calls and the length of these calls you understand why. There is always someone who is a talk junky, one who stays on the thing for hours. Consider cancelling the landline altogether and switch to a mobile. Opt for a pay as you go if your family members tend to be heavy mobile phone users.

Here's what the Dunne family did:

> They had one landline with a broadband package and five mobile phones! When they added up their phone bills and the amounts spent on pay as you go phones the total came to €400! That's €4800 a year – not an uncommon figure. Within a week they had switched telephone provider and got rid of three mobile phones, saving €300 per month.

You will be unsurprised to know I'm a mobile junkie and I'll talk for Ireland. In 2008 my mobile phone bill was running

at €450 per month! I'd love to tell you I logged on to www.
callcosts.ie and did a comparison of competing mobile
packages but I didn't. Instead I consulted my fifteen-year-
old son and that same day he accompanied me into a phone
shop where I switched providers and signed up to a fixed
charge of €100 per month, saving more than €4000 a year.
I felt like a right clod as I'm supposed to know this stuff. My
son doesn't let me forget it either, every time he's looking for
something extra!

Energy Savings

The price of oil and gas will stay depressed during the global
downturn, but the margin between supply and demand is
so tight that the first sign of economic improvement will
bring a return to sharply-rising prices, although without
the speculative bubble that brought oil to a record $147 per
barrel in 2008. It is possible that Ireland will still be deep
in recession when commodity costs begin to rise again, so
anything you can do today, whether buying new bulbs or
getting into new habits, will pay dividends tomorrow. One
you get started it becomes easy to use energy more efficiently
in your daily life. Here are some useful tips that will prove
even more useful when oil and gas prices rebound.

Turn your heating down to a comfortable 20ºC – lowering
your thermostat by 1ºC will knock 10% off your heating bill.
Why not turn it down by two degrees and wear a jumper?

- It's not too long ago since most houses were heated by
  coal fires and we all went to bed in cold rooms with hot-
  water bottles. How many bedrooms are heated in your
  house? If you live in a two-storey house, why would you

want to heat the all bedrooms? Hot air rises. Try it – it does work.

- Consider replacing your open fireplace with a stove. These stoves throw off the most fantastic heat

- If you have an older house built from cavity blocks investigate the possibility of having insulation beads injected into the walls by an expert. I had this done on an exposed house built in the late 1970s and the improvement was remarkable.

- Increase your attic insulation to the modern re-commended standard, about quadruple the thickness of yesteryear.

- Invest in double- or triple-glazed windows if you have the funds.

- When buying kitchen stuff buy 'A' appliances. They cost less to run and in time will give you considerable savings on your electricity bill. Appliances with the highest ratings may cost a little more but this will pay for itself in time.

- Use compact fluorescent lamps (CFLs) instead of trad-itional bulbs. They use 20% of the energy and last for up to fifteen times as long.

- Wait for the dishwasher to be full before you switch it on. A half-full one uses the same energy as a full one.The same is true for washing machines where most clothes can be washed on quick cycles at 40 degrees.

- Switch off lights when you leave a room. Energy is wasted lighting unoccupied rooms.

- Think fitness. Why not walk or cycle short journeys instead of driving.

- Check your tyre pressure. A car with correctly inflated tyres is more fuel-efficient. Close the windows when driving. Reduce your speed to 80 kmh and switch off the air conditioning.

- Don't overfill your kettle. Boil only as much water as you need.
- Unplug your phone charger and other equipment. Equipment on standby uses up to 20% of the energy it would use when fully turned on.

Get the Energy Grants

Sustainable Energy Ireland (www.SEI.ie), overseen by Environment Minister Eamon Ryan of the Green Party, has made available a range of grants for which you may qualify, to turn your home into a real energy-saving investment over the years ahead. Of particular benefit are the grants available to people on low incomes, including those dependent on social welfare, but other grants are now rolling out, supported by a €100 million injection by the National Development Plan. You may qualify for grants to help with installing basic technology like cavity-wall injection or advanced technology like solar panels. Find out what you qualify for and make sure you apply pronto. Visit www.SEI.ie today.

Help for Pensioners and the Low-Paid

Even if your own home is well insulated, the chances that are your parents are living in a poorly-insulated house built in the 1960s or 1970s. Unless these have been upgraded they'll be riddled with draughts and, with inadequate attic insulation and cavity walls free of any type of modern insulation, will find it difficult to hold heat for very long. The SEI Warmer Homes Scheme, administered through a nationwide network, is a cracker for those on low incomes, typically those on social welfare and pensioners who would otherwise be unable to stump up the full commercial cost of insulating their homes. Following a review of your home and your means, a wide range of treatments is available at very modest costs. These include: attic insulation to top standards, cavity-wall injection, draught-proofing, energy-efficient lighting and even lagging jackets. This is a must scheme for any household that qualifies. You can find out more about it on http://www.sei.ie/Grants/Warmer_Homes_Scheme/.

The Greener Homes Scheme

SEI also offers a variety of grants if you want to make your home greener. If you intend to purchase a new renewable-energy heating system, it's worth checking out SEI's 'approved installer' list on www.sei.ie/greenerhomes. If you have an approved product installed by an approved installer you will qualify for the following grants:

- Biomass: Installing a biomass boiler nets an impressive €2500 from SEI, a biomass-based stove earns a grant of €800, and a biomass stove with an integral back boiler nabs you €1400.
- Heat pumps: Heat pump systems attract some of the most generous grants on offer. A vertical ground system is eligible for a grant of up to €3500, with €2500 awarded for a horizontal ground or water-to-water system. An air-source system qualifies for a grant of €2000.
- Solar Panels: Two varieties of solar panels are eligible for grants. Flat-plate panels are eligible for €250 per metre squared, while evacuated tube panels attract €300 per metre squared. Both grants are subject to a maximum of six metres squared.

- Burning wood: A wood gasification boiler, which uses wood for energy in a particularly efficient way, qualifies for an award of €2000 from SEI.

There are some terms and conditions, though: you can qualify for only one grant under the scheme and, if you availed of a grant under phase one or two of the scheme, you can't claim again!

The Home Energy Saving Scheme

SEI have issued details of the roll-out of the Home Energy Saving Scheme after its €5m pilot. This is supported by €100 million as part of the National Development Plan. The scheme was originally announced in April 2008 by Energy Minister Eamon Ryan. The pilot scheme targeted older housing, as these homes are most in need of energy-efficiency retrofitting. A Building Energy Rating (BER) assessor comes to your home to give a BER rating and advise on the works that need to be carried out to improve energy efficiency. Under the pilot scheme you pre-pay €100 towards the cost of this assessment, with SEI subsidising the remaining two-thirds. The assessor may advise that your house requires such work as attic insulation, interior or exterior wall insulation, low emissions double-glazing, heating control or a range of other energy efficient works. You then get a grant to cover up to 30% of the cost of these works, to a maximum of €2,500. On completion of the works an assessor will carry out a follow-up energy assessment on the building. Minster Ryan reckons that of the 1.7 million homes in Ireland, up to one million require some investment to improve their energy efficiency and that householders will thereby save on their electricity and heating bills, use energy more wisely and increase the resale value of their homes. SEI estimate that families could save up to €500 in energy bills every year, that the pilot scheme will save 6,000 tonnes of CO_2 in its first year alone and that a full roll-out of the €100 million scheme will yield greenhouse gas savings of 175,000 tonnes per year. The full scheme was announced in the spring of 2009. Check out www.SEI.ie for details of the grants that will be available. They will include:

- €250 for roof insulations
- €400 for cavity-wall insulation
- €2500 for internal dry-lining of walls
- €4000 of external wall insulation
- €700 for the installation of a high-efficiency gas/oil burner
- €500 for the upgrade of heating controls
- €200 for BER assessment

Insurance

Don't accept any renewal premium at face value. Go online or get on the phone and get quotes from competitors. If you get a cheaper quote phone your insurer and ask them to match it. Threaten to move and see what happens. Try to bundle your house and car insurance – you might get a better rate on both. Do you really need the kids on your insurance? Can they walk or cycle? There are large savings to be made if you have money problems. Can you sell the big car and get a smaller car that will be cheaper to insure and tax?

Here's a real cracker of a money-saving idea. One of the few benefits of a collapse in asset prices, both for homes and cars is – guess what? – cheaper house and motor insurance! Remember how the insurance companies were always reminding you to make sure your house was properly valued for fire and building insurance in the rising property market? Well, don't be surprised if they're not as enthusiastic in writing out to you to alert you to falling prices because their premiums and profits will suffer. Adjust your building insurance policy now to reflect the true value of your property. If you were over-insured in 2008 you might even get a refund of premium – it won't hurt to ask. The same goes for motor insurance. The bottom has fallen out of the used-car market so at renewal check the resale price of your car, jeep or motorbike and ask your insurers to adjust your premium downwards.

Christmas

Nobody does Christmas like the Irish. The average Irish family spends €1,400, twice as much as our European neighbours, on the same Christian holiday. But how do you save cash? For starters look at all the food we eat – we consume 6,000 calories on Christmas day alone. Then look at all the food we buy that we end up throwing out. Why not buy a fourteen-pound turkey this Christmas instead of trying to fit a twenty-pound monster into your oven. The same goes for ham: remember that throwing out expensive food is the same as opening your wallet or handbag and emptying the contents into the bin. Factor in the champagne, wine and spirits and it all adds up to lots of waste. This Christmas, write up a budget in advance – not just for all the food and drink but for gifts – and stick to it. If you haven't yet organised a Kris Kindle this is the year to do it. Try shopping for presents throughout the year. The best time for bargains in Christmas items, like decorations, lighting and tableware, is at the beginning of the January sales, when shops offload surplus stock.

Booze and Fags

Not surprisingly, the greatest saving can be made in cutting back or eliminating the old reliables. About 20% of the population smokes and most of us drink our heads off all year around with a slight dip during Lent! When I presented *Show Me The Money* the typical spend on stuff we push through our lungs and livers was typically between 10% and 20% of the net income of over-spenders – and not just carefree singletons. It may give you quite a shock to tot up the cost of six-packs and wine at home and add what you spend in pubs and on booze trips away disguised as overseas sporting events. I'm no killjoy and I love my wines, but limiting your weekly intake of alcohol isn't just good for your health and your energy, especially as you get older – it can save you a bundle of cash too.

TV Services

Top-priced TV services like Sky that include a very limited number of high-definition programmes cost about €500 per year. Ask yourself: did you sign up under pressure from the kids? Look at the small number of channels they watch these days as they migrate towards games and the Internet. Admit it: pricey TV services are a luxury. There are lots of standard channels available via a satellite dish that you can buy and install cheaply.

Fees and Commissions

Watch out for services that charge a percentage, common in the area of property, and negotiate flat fees instead.

Conveyance solicitors and architects are especially fond of charging for their services as a percentage of the property value, your extension or new-build. Pension and investment salespeople still mostly charge you as a percentage of your first-year contribution. You're entitled to commission disclosure but it's not universally available and often deeply buried in small print. Insist on disclosure upfront and ideally negotiate a fee for work done instead of a standard commission.

Petrol and Home-Heating Oil

Oil prices are in a temporary trough due to the global drop in demand as a result of contractions in the US, European and many other OECD economies. But even though a fill of petrol or home heating is down from the peaks of 2008 when oil hit $147 a barrel, prices for consumer products vary considerably. Make a habit of using the cheapest petrol stations in your area. If you're nearly dry and forced into a high-priced station don't fill up the tank – just get enough to get you to your favoured supplier. The same applies to home heating refills. Phone around or go online. You will be shocked at the price difference.

Tax Refunds

Make sure you're claiming all your allowances and expenses against your tax. Tax experts reckon that the average Irish taxpayer leaves behind about €500 in unclaimed reliefs on waste charges, rents, medical and dental expenses and mortgages, among other things. Check out the Revenue Commissioners' website, Revenue.ie

Charities

You can support charities without hitting your tight cash. Old mobile phones, personal computers and ink cartridges may have no value for you but organisations like the Jack and Jill Foundation will turn your waste into cash. This in turn will provide paediatric nurses who deliver support to Irish families with babies requiring twenty-four hour care. Phone Jack and Jill on 1850-524554.

15

Coping with Job-Loss

In a boom labour market there was nearly always a silver lining if you lost your job: a nice lump of cash in your hand, a few weeks off and another job just around the corner. It was easy to feel confident – the newspapers had beefy supplements with pages of jobs backed by websites offering thousands more. But all that has changed. Then you might have expected to spend at most three to four months' job-hunting. Now it is likely to take far longer to find a new job.

If you have lost your job or are facing redundancy – although you may be very lucky and bounce back quickly – the best thing you can do right now is to plan. The worst thing you can to is do nothing but burn through your cash and hide from your debt until it escalates into a problem you may not be able to control.

Ned Maloney lost his job in April 2008 when his employer, a big building-supply·firm, was forced to cut employment numbers by a third. Developers had started to run out of cash and were resorting to paying invoices by instalments. Cheques were beginning to bounce. As the company marketing manager Ned was defenceless and surplus to requirements. His employers put their hands deep into the company reserves and paid redundancy lump sums well above statutory minimums.

Almost a year later Ned is still looking for a job that matches his skillset. Like many other professionals who had a good job with a strong salary, he is now finding it hard to get meaningful work. Used to earning €120,000, including a €10,000 contribution to his pension fund, he made only token changes to the family's lifestyle, never visualising that he might be jobless a year later. Like many in his sector, he believed in the doctrine of the temporary dip before Ireland's insatiable appetite for property would recover. He finds that his redundancy lump sum of €50,000 and the family savings are close to being exhausted, and his wife is searching for a part-time job to keep them ticking over. Ned now realises that he was a classic case of someone who believes they will find work at the same salary level and continues living as he has always done – including going on holidays.

The family is facing very severe cutbacks in spending and Ned has to put together a debt-repayment proposal for their mortgage and car loans. He is kicking himself because he knows he could have stretched the family's assets out for at least another year with a bit more prudence and foresight.

Ned's story contains an important message. If you're one of the many people facing the loss of your job, it is best to plan for a much longer jobless period than during the past number of years, whether or not another income is coming into the home. That means putting a twenty-four-month plan in place instead of one for six months. Better to err on the side of caution today and slowly burn through available cash than blow it over a few short months in a forlorn attempt to maintain your lifestyle for the benefit of neighbours and friends. Remember it will take an austerity programme and at least two years before Ireland returns to growth, so you should plan accordingly. If, in the meantime, you manage to get one-off projects that bring in some cash or if you land some kind of job, that's a bonus. But just about the worst thing you can do is to pretend nothing much has changed – even though that's a perfectly understandable human reaction.

So what should you do? The first thing to do when you hear that your job is going is to take immediate stock of where you are financially. Do up a statement of affairs as suggested earlier. That means starting with a balance sheet summarising everything you own and you owe and then prepare an income and expenditure analysis for the next two years at least.

Find a good home for your lump sum, paying the best possible interest rate. Because lots of Irish consumers are not willing to take time to shop around, half of all the money on deposit with banks earns only half the maximum possible interest. Time to squeeze the best you can out of the market. For instance, in early 2009, Northern Rock, now 100% British-government owned, was paying interest for on-line and on-demand deposits at double the ECB base rate. Competition changes, so shop around. Keep an eye on information from the Financial Regulator – www. itsyourmoney.ie – or check out the money chat website www.askaboutmoney.ie.

When you are preparing your budget, pay particular attention to the discipline of separating necessary from optional spending. When you calculate your available cash from liquid assets and divide it by necessary monthly spending, you can then estimate how long you can keep going with the adjusted lifestyle you have identified. You may also be entitled to support payment from the state. If you happen to get extra cash, from odd jobs or short-term contracts, rework the figures before using the extra money to enhance your lifestyle. After calculating the level of support you need to plug the gap left by your state benefits and any other family income, transfer this amount from your lump sum deposit account to your main bank account once a month. This is the income you're paying yourself from liquid assets. Don't forget to adjust for irregular big bills – see the section called 'When Big Bills Frighten You' on page 52 and Appendix 4.

Don't Put Budgeting on the Long Finger

People often make the critical mistake of putting off the unpleasant task of examining their lifestyle and budgeting until after they take the holiday they always wanted. Ask anyone who has been working hard with nothing longer than a fortnight off for years and who faces redundancy. They will tell you that the first thing they want to do is to take a month off and do nothing. For some people this means a month during which they will look around for other jobs and network and plan while playing golf, but for others this month off is fatal. Being idle saps the energy, lethargy sets in and before you know it the month off has stretched out to six months. This is demoralising and breaks the habit of work.

So get cracking on the household budget. Don't wait until the fateful day when you have no work to go to. You need to know what the impact of a loss of income will be. Use the budget form in Appendix 1 or any other one that works – the important thing is to do it.

Pay Off Short-term Debt First

When you have completed your statement of affairs, look closely at your short-term debt, like credit cards, overdrafts and store cards. This is the most expensive debt. Pay off these balances immediately; otherwise, at double-digit interest rates, they will drain your cash. It's a mistake to leave short-term loans intact and pay them as usual because it reinforces the unwise assumption that you will be back to work in jig time and that there is no reason to repay these loans now. It's fantastic to be confident and upbeat in the face of adversity like a job loss but optimism is no substitute for good financial husbandry.

Ideally scrap all credit cards and use cash cards instead, but if you feel you must keep one, retain the card with the lowest limit. Use the card for making payments but not for financing anything that you cannot afford to buy today from your savings. Remember you do not have regular income and are using your savings to live. Preferably decide to buy an item for cash or not at all.

Loan Protection Insurance

Look closely at the fine-print of your loan agreements. If you have lost them ask the lender for a copy. Check to see if you were sold loan-protection insurance for your mortgage or other loans. The lender who may have quietly slipped this insurance in during the sales patter when you were signing up will have no idea that you're facing a job loss; neither will the insurer. Neither is in the habit of writing out to policy-holders to remind them to make a claim. These insurances are integrated with your monthly repayments and unless you have scrutinised your statements closely you may have missed them. The cheaper types of loan protection can cover your repayments for up to two years in the event of sickness or accident and the more expensive type extend to cover redundancy. You should act quickly as these policies have strict application deadlines, after which you will lose the redundancy cover.

If you find you have such loan-protection insurance, insist on seeing a copy of the policy document before completing a claim. The chances are you were never given a copy: a group policy may be held centrally by the lender. You could be pleasantly surprised. If there's any tomfoolery in processing your claim don't be slow to make a written complaint to the Office of the Financial Services Ombudsman, a free arbitration service whose rulings are binding on the insurer.

Keep Fit Cheaply

Keeping fit when you're jobless is good for your energy levels and morale. If your passion is cycling, hiking, running or hunting there's no point in maintaining costly club memberships you hardly use. Look closely at cost per use. If your annual gym or golf-club fee is €1000 and you use it only five times a year, the cost per use is €200. You could be better off cancelling the membership and paying day or green fees.

School Fees

Parents will move heaven and earth to get their children a good education but that doesn't mean you can't be practical about it. Perhaps the hottest subject is private versus public education – whether paying out up to €15,000 a year in fees makes sense. It's pretty academic if you're at work and you can maintain private fees or boarding costs but when you don't have the cash, family survival takes priority. Be proactive: talk to the school principal about paying lower fees or skipping them entirely for a year. You can be pretty sure you will get a sympathetic and confidential hearing because all private schools are now dealing with parents who can't afford to pay. And even if you eventually have no choice but to pull the kids out of private schools, remember most kids are very adaptable and resettle easily. Most of the problem may be your own ego. Remember you're broke: you're not poor. A broke person dusts himself down and gets going again. As for the educational standards – well, there's lots of evidence that non-fee-paying schools are mighty handy at getting the best out of the kids they educate and are teeming with superb teachers.

For what it's worth I went to Coláiste Chríost Rí in Turner's Cross in Cork, a publicly-funded GAA-orientated school. Some of my friends went to fee-paying private rugby schools, Pres and Christians. I didn't because we couldn't afford it. I played rugby without distinction at Highfield RFC and had a blast! At Coláiste Chríost Rí I had access to some of the finest teachers in the city for English, Maths, French and the Sciences and I'm certain that many schools throughout the country have similar strong cultures of good free education. Lots of my pals at Coláiste Chríost Rí got excellent Leaving Certificate results and went on to carve out careers in medicine, business and the sciences.

Fees aside, many ancillary costs can creep up on you. Carry out an accurate assessment of the monthly cost of sending a child to school, including books, music lessons and the cost of lunches from the nearby shop or takeout. Switching to packed lunches will save you a lot of money and be healthier for the kids. If you have to drive your children to school talk to other parents about pooling cars for school and after-school trips. There's an industry involved in producing schoolbooks which, like soccer jerseys, are changed year by year. The cost of buying books for a first year secondary-school student is estimated at €400-€500. There are many areas in which school management and parents' councils could focus on cost-reduction, particularly with regard to the hidden schooling costs such as books. Why not establish a book-exchange programme in your children's school?

Stay Busy

The first few weeks of joblessness are critically important in establishing a pattern of healthy habits such as getting up as normal with the rest of the family and treating each day as a project to sniff out opportunities to earn cash and look for a job. If you don't do this, you are in danger of establishing an unhealthy routine that could undermine your confidence and lead to despondency.

Tactics for the
Long-distance Job-hunter

It's pretty tough when savings get eroded because of unemployment and debts become distressed. Remember you are not alone – tens of thousands of people are in the same boat, not just in Ireland. There is nothing 'wrong' with you. You will work again. It may take some time but it will happen. In the meantime dust down the CV and begin the process of job-hunting.

Resources are available online and there are plenty of good books that advise you what to do. The main tip is to make time – real job-hunting is a job in itself. And start straight away. Don't treat unemployment like an extended holiday. If there's no chance of finding work locally that's suitable for your skills locally, investigate getting retrained. Register with FÁS and find out about the range of back-to-work courses. You may be surprised at the range of training available.

Once you are finished job-hunting for the day move on to something else. It may be cutting the grass, going for a walk or helping the kids with their homework – but it is not job-hunting. There is nothing more soul-destroying then constantly worrying about finding a job as well as worrying about money. If you think of yourself as a victim, you will become a victim and begin to live in an internal world where your feelings could spiral into depression.

You can only do so much. If you haven't the money, you haven't the money. Nothing is simpler than this. If you haven't the income to repay all you owe when it comes due then what you have is a problem with money. It is not a problem with you or your worthiness or integrity as a person. It's only money. Remember that your other assets far outweigh the money problem. You have your health. You have your family. You have a network of supporters that may be much larger than you think.

List everyone you know. Tell them you are looking for a job and ask for their help. People like to be asked and most people will help if they can. Repaying distressed debt will take time. It may take years to repay loans and bills but they will eventually be cleared or written off. How you choose to deal with the problem depends on you. You can retreat into feelings of uselessness and despair or you can recognise that all that matters are your health and the health of those you live with. Everyone is different. The lucky few are engineered for adversity and relish the challenge but most of us mortals need to draw strength from others.

State Support when You Are Jobless

This is a brief overview of the key benefits. To understand the detail of some of the complex rules that surround state benefits there is one key piece of independent writing, *Know Your Rights* by Andrew McCann, that I recommend highly. Andrew, who works for Fingal Citizens' Information Service, is not just an expert but one of those gems who is passionate about helping people and sharing his knowledge. His book is a treasure.

There are two main allowances. If you are aged eighteen or over and unemployed you may be paid either jobseeker's allowance or jobseeker's benefit payments by the Department of Social and Family Affairs. Jobseeker's allowance was once called unemployment assistance and jobseeker's benefit was called unemployment benefit.

If you have been on PAYE and made PRSI contributions, jobseeker's benefit is paid on a sliding scale for up to twelve months, depending on how long you have been making PRSI contributions and your average earnings. It's a taxable non-means-tested payment. If you are under the age of fifty-five and receive a redundancy payment of more than €50,000 you will be disqualified from claiming the benefit for up to nine weeks.

You may get jobseeker's allowance if you don't qualify for jobseeker's benefit or if you have used up your entitlement to jobseeker's benefit. In some cases, if you are only entitled to a reduced rate of jobseeker's benefit, you may be better off on jobseeker's allowance. However, jobseeker's allowance is means-tested and your means must be below a certain level for you to qualify.

As of February 2009, the maximum jobseeker's benefit and allowance payments are:

Person	Payment €	Qualifying Criteria (Benefit)
You	204.30 per week	PRSI contributions and earnings
Your partner	135.60 per week	Earnings
Your dependent child	26.00 per week	None

The maximum jobseeker's benefit payment for a family of two adults and three dependent children where the sole earner has become unemployed is €417.90 for a period of twelve months.

If you are self-employed you will not qualify for benefit but may qualify for the allowance. You may qualify for either payment if you are on reduced income. Detailed rules apply both to benefit and allowance and you should check the resources listed below.

When You Become Unemployed

Go to your local social welfare office and apply for jobseeker's benefit or jobseeker's allowance, bringing two forms of identification and your P45, P60 and redundancy notice. If you don't have these documents to hand, apply anyway to protect your entitlements.

Once your claim is registered you may have to wait if there is a claims backlog. If you have no other income you can in the meantime apply to the community welfare officer at your local health centre for a supplementary welfare allowance payment, which is means-tested. If you are paying a mortgage or rent you may be entitled to a mortgage-interest supplement or rent supplement.

A range of additional supports is also available, including:

- Smokeless fuel allowance
- Back-to-school clothing and footwear
- Medical card
- School book scheme

Social Welfare rules are complicated and take some getting used to. The good news is that excellent resources are available at local social welfare offices and health centres.

- Detailed information is available at www.welfare.ie.
- MABS and Citizens Information Centres – www. citizensinformation.ie – also provide information and advice.
- *Know Your Rights* by Andrew McCann (published by Blackhall) is available from any good bookshop.

Your Redundancy Rights

If you are losing your job because your employer is closing down or reducing staff numbers you are being made redundant and you are entitled to a statutory redundancy payment if you have worked for this employer for a certain period of time, currently set at two years' continuous service. You are entitled to two weeks' pay for every year of service with a bonus week added, up to a ceiling of €600 gross weekly pay. For example, if you have worked for a company for ten years you would be entitled to a maximum payment of €12,600. Your employer claims a rebate of 60% of the cost from the government. Minimum statutory redundancy is tax-exempt.

Tax and Redundancy

You are entitled to certain tax allowances that will reduce the tax liability on your redundancy payment.

Basic Exemption	€10,160
Years' service	€765 per year
Additional Exemption	€10,000

For example:

Orla has worked for her company for eight years and is being paid a redundancy lump sum of €30,000. Her non-taxable portion is €10,160+8 x €765.00 = €16,280. The balance of €13,720 is taxed as income. If Orla is a member of the company's pension scheme and agrees to give up her right to take a lump sum at retirement, an additional €10,000 tax-free allowance applies. In this case, she will be taxed on only €3720.

An alternative method of liability calculation can be used for high earners who were taxed at the higher marginal rate. Called Standard Capital Superannuation Benefit (SCSB), it takes the average annual earnings over the previous three years and multiplies this average by the number of years of service. This is divided by fifteen and the amount of the lump sum received is subtracted from the result. Sounds complex? Here's an example:

John has earned €100,000 a year for the past three years. His redundancy scheme is seven weeks' pay per year and he has worked for ten years with his company. This means his lump sum is €100,000÷52 x 7 x 10 = €134,615.

Options	(a) Basic Exemption €	(b) SCSB
Income	100,000	100,000
Redundancy Lump sum	134,615	134,615
Tax-Free Element	17,810	66,666
Amount to Be Taxed	116,805	67,949

Clearly John should opt for the SCSB approach as this reduces the taxable element of his lump sum.

Finally there is an additional relief called Top Slicing Relief. It ensures that your lump sum is not taxed at a rate higher than your average rate of tax for the past three years.

Here's how this one works:

In John's case the taxable element of his lump sum is €67,949 at his marginal tax rate of 41%. But his average tax rate for the previous three years was 33%. The difference between the two rates is 8% so John's tax payable will be reduced by 8% or €5435.00.

Depending on when you are made redundant in a tax year you will benefit from your full year's tax credits. In John's case the portion of his lump sum that is liable for tax will be taxed at 41% in the month it is paid, but if he does not work for the rest of the year he can use his outstanding tax credits to reclaim some of the tax paid.

The examples here have been simplified to show the effect of tax reliefs on redundancy lump sum payments. You should access the resources below for more detail of how the system works. If you are being made redundant it is likely that your employer will provide advice and assistance on tax and pension consequences.

Finally, redundancy affects your pension entitlements. This is a complex area to which you will need to give careful consideration. You will need professional advice on the area and if your employer does not provide this you should consult an independent pensions consultant who is familiar with redundancy issues.

Resources
- 'Guide to the Redundancy Payments Scheme': www.entemp.ie/publications/employment/2004/
- 'Lump Sum Payments (redundancy/retirement)' T21: www.revenue.ie
- 'Pensions Manual': www.revenue.ie
- Citizens Information Centres www.citizensinformation.ie.

16

Be Aware of Depression

Losing your job is traumatic, right up there among life's most stressful feelings of loss. As with any loss, everybody's reaction will be different. If you don't quite grasp the almost euphoric enthusiasm displayed by a colleague giddy at the prospect of freedom or the optimism of some American self-help guru you see on television, this doesn't make your feelings invalid. You might be much better off in the long run feeling some grief now rather than vainly trying to suppress it – that is, as long as you get through the grief period and out the other side to take on the world again, not as you'd like it to be but as it is.

This is tricky ground – after all I'm working – so let me get one thing into the open: except for a few months very early in my career I have never been unemployed. The manager of a local supermarket once fired me aggressively from a part-time job, thinking that was a big joke to fire a youngster in front of the rest of the staff, but that's it for me. But I do know what it's like to live in a home with a parent suffering from long-term depression. My own father, another Eddie, died in 1983 at the young age of fifty-two, from a heart attack brought on by depression, smoking and weight-loss. He had suffered from very bad depression for fourteen years, during which time he was mostly at work, although he did have periods of unemployment. He never had a bright day during his illness but went out every day to face customers all over Munster. He did his job as a commercial traveller to support his family, returning home in the evening to collapse into bed early. He cried a lot. I have no hesitation in saying that my dad was a hero.

The worst thing that can happen if you have distressed debt or lose your job is that you become depressed. Depression is silent and unseen but creates feelings of uselessness and hopelessness, even despair. The impact of job-loss, loss of connectedness to society and worries about money can have really serious psychological consequences.

Suicide rates increase during deep recessions and whilst there is no systematic analysis that points to debt and job-loss as the cause, they are undoubtedly contributory factors. Those who work in helping people struggle with the burden of debt all speak of the loss of self-esteem and feelings of hopelessness that affect entire families. Even professionals working in debt counselling are prone to feelings of despondency as they try to help people to deal with debt and the resultant depression. I found out many years later that my father's GP also suffered from depression!

Depression can still be stigmatised in Irish society although, largely as a result of the campaigning work of AWARE, the organisation for those suffering from depression and their families, people are now talking more openly about their depression and public awareness of the condition is on the increase.

Recognise Depression if It Visits

You're certainly not alone if you have a depressive episode, as it is estimated that at any one time about 300,000 people in Ireland are suffering from some kind of depression. So get help. It is not necessarily a good idea to trying to struggle on courageously in the silence of your own mind. The good news is that depression is now understood to be an illness from which the vast majority of people recover quite quickly.

Here's one man's story:

I lost my job in 2007 when the company I worked for closed down its Irish operations. Mind you, my redundancy payment was quite good and came to about six months' net salary after I had availed of the tax breaks. We had put savings in the bank over the years – about €20,000 – and as well as our mortgage of €80,000 I had a car loan of €15,000. I thought I would get another job quite quickly as I'm well qualified and have worked for more than twenty years in the same industry. Little did I realise how tough it would be.

I am still unemployed and what little we have left will see us through about three months, after which the only income we will have is the dole. My biggest regret is that I took things too easy, believing a job was around the corner. As the weeks and then months went by and CV after CV was rejected, I fell into a routine at home. I did little except worry and fret about finding a job and helping with the housework. My wife went back to work so I took over as the main home-minder. This became my routine. Gradually I noticed that I stayed in my dressing gown longer every day after the children had gone to school. A feeling of loss and hopelessness set in and I felt as if I was all alone with no future and began to feel worthless. I didn't know it but I was depressed and began to withdraw from my friends who remained working.

After a while their calls dropped off, as we had little or nothing to talk of save their work. My family know there was something wrong but my own pride and fear prevented me from looking for help. When I was asked how things were going I would try to change the subject and not talk about how I was feeling or how hard it was for me not to work. I was short-tempered with my children and my wife and became a bit of an angry dog, barking at the slightest problem. My despondency caused my world to shrink to the garden and then the house itself, which became a cosy prison I locked myself into away from a world I felt I no longer contributed to.

That is until I started thinking about not being around any more, imagining what life would be like for my family if I was gone. I even started thinking about how to die without too much of a mess. I reasoned that although my family would be upset by my death, they would eventually move on with their own lives. I calculated how much they would have to live on and factored in the little life insurance we had.

Thankfully I got a chance call from an old friend who'd heard I'd lost my job. He'd been through something similar and I'd forgotten it completely. I should have rung him immediately. Anyway we met for coffee and he described precisely what I was feeling inside. I thought I was the only one who'd ever been through these feelings. After meeting him I talked to a counsellor over about four sessions. I realised I needed help and went and got some. It is still hard to wake up and know the day will not be the same without work but now I believe in myself again and am beginning to go out more. I know now that it is possible I may never again have a job like I had or enjoy the same lifestyle or if we do it will take longer to get there than next month. But I am happier. I'm prepared to change and adapt to the way things work out and I'm putting in some voluntary work with the local elderly. I still have the off-day when I do feel despondent but I know what to do now – get off my butt and get on with something.

Depression isn't like a flu that announces its arrival with blocked sinuses, fatigue and coughing. It's more of a sneaky illness that can creep up on you to invade your mental and physical health without your realising it. That's why knowing the symptoms is vital. They can now be identified as a collection, much like a collection of symptoms that might identify heart disease. AWARE has done much to make society familiar with these symptoms, including inventing a handy mnemonic, *festival*:

- Feelings: depressed, sad, anxious or bored
- Energy: tired, fatigued, everything an effort, slowed movements
- Sleep: waking during the night or too early in the morning, oversleeping or having trouble getting to sleep
- Thinking: slow thinking, poor concentration, being forgetful or indecisive
- Interest: loss of interest in food, work, sex, and life seems dull
- Value: reduced sense of self-worth, low self-esteem or guilt
- Aches: headaches, chest or other pains without a physical basis
- Live: not wanting to live, suicidal thoughts or thinking of death

You don't have to feel depressed to be depressed. If you are suffering from five or more of the above symptoms for more than two weeks, see your GP without hesitation.

In 1985, two years after my father's death, AWARE was formed to provide emotional support for those who experience depression and their families. It seeks to create increased public awareness of the nature, extent and consequences of depressive illness – hence the name. AWARE also promotes research into causes and effective treatment of mood disorder. I would like to thank the organisation for its help in covering this topic in the book and for fulfilling such a badly-needed role in Irish society.

AWARE reminds us that depression is a treatable illness. It can be disabling as it affects our thinking, feeling and behaviour. It is often described as an overwhelming feeling which dulls thinking, impairs concentration, saps energy, interest in food, sex, work and daily events and also disrupts sleep. Depression affects one in four of us at some point in our lives and women are three to four times more likely to suffer from it than men. Left untreated, depression can prove fatal, resulting in the tragedy of suicide. There are different, very distinct types and the most likely to accompany job loss is *reactive* depression. Once again, thanks to AWARE for this description:

Reactive depression is a reaction to an unhappy event in a person's life, such as bereavement, relationship breakdown or loss of employment. The individual will typically feel low, anxious, angry or irritable and will often be preoccupied with the upsetting event. We all place different importance on events, so something which may be deemed minor by one person can be a major trauma for another.

Reactive depression differs from *endogenous* depression, which is primarily a biological or inherited condition, although disappointment may trigger it.

If you are feeling depressed or despairing, only you can do something about it. Seek help from your doctor or a counsellor. There is absolutely nothing to fear. Unchecked depression does lead to physical illness that can be fatal.

17

What's Next?

Nobody knows precisely when we'll come out of this recession. The science of economics is simply too imprecise to cope with all the variables, and forecasts are always wrong – it's just a question of by how much. As ever, there are two opposing voices. During the boom the bulls held sway – the optimists who reckoned that things could only get better. Right now the loudest voices are the bears', the pessimists who think we're in for a very deep and prolonged recession, in other words a depression. For what it's worth I don't buy into that.

Despite what media headlines would have you believe, the current recession is very different from the 1930s, when there was a huge contraction in cash and governments slashed spending. During the valuation-bubble burst of 2000-03 – after hugely inflated prices had been paid for companies such as dot.coms – the US government staved off multi-year recession by aggressive interest-rate cuts and tax rebates. The credit bubble underneath continued to expand, and economic growth between 2003 and 2008 was artificial. This time we're seeing an earnings-bubble burst as businesses throughout the world realise that they cannot achieve their forecasted expansion in earnings, as so much of their sales was contingent on customers having freely-available credit. The result is a sharp worldwide fall in asset-values in property, shares and commodities, as businesses and consumers begin the painful process of reducing their debts and building up their cash. In other words, what's happening is a natural part of the economic cycle. All that is different this time are the speed and extent of the recession because of the globalised nature of the modern world, integrated global banking markets and the failure to regulate the market properly. As ever, humanity is learning from its mistakes on the job.

It is a very short while since the tumultuous events of September 2008 when the world faced the possibility of a banking collapse. It is going to take time before counter-measures take effect. While the consensus is for a return to fragile growth in 2010 in major economic regions like the US and Europe, the speed and strength of the recovery could yet catch us by surprise. I put my faith in human behaviour – in enterprise and greed replacing caution and fear.

A gigantic dam of cash, from asset sell-offs and savings, has built up on the sidelines. These trillions of dollars, Euro and yen are earning close to nothing in banks and government bonds. Inevitably the dam will crack and then burst as investors rush out to take advantage of fantastic value in companies, property, commodities and new busi-nesses. This will fire the next cycle. There's plenty of reason to be hopeful if you look beyond media headlines and lagging indicators like rising unemployment and business closures to green shoots, the leading indicators of recovery.

Despite the overwhelming mood of despondency gripping the country and understandable criticism of govern-ment failure to act quickly, Ireland may yet follow the US out of recession faster than forecasted because of the very open nature of the Irish economy. Of course there is a great deal to be done and much pain to be endured along the way, especially in driving down costs, correcting unaffordable public spending and repairing over-geared balance sheets, but that was already underway by early 2009. The key is leadership: people who know the way, show the way and go the way. Ireland isn't going down the tubes and neither are you.

A recession is as natural to economic cycles as snow and rain are to weather. It may seem as if your life will never be the same again and this may be true – it could be better. Tightening up on spending now, even negotiating debt write-downs, is a phase. It won't last forever. Once you're through it, even if you're out of work for a time, you can start all over again. That's the story of economic cycles; that's the story of humanity.

There's one banner I always love to see. You'll find it at every Munster rugby match and it carries just one word: *believe.*

Appendix 1
Spending Budget

Put your pre-budget monthly spend in column 1. Put your adjusted spend in column 2. Use column 3 for any notes.

To start, use your best guess when you're not sure. Afterwards you will have to run a cash diary for at least a month and ideally three months to validate casual cash expenditures. These are highlighted with (?). The rest should be obvious from credit card bills, cheque stubs and bank statements – direct debits and standing orders. Start with the records you can check easily. Ideally look over the last twelve months if you still have the records.

	Expenditure Analysis	What Has Been Spent Monthly €	What Will Be Spent Monthly €	Notes
1.	Housekeeping Expenses			
	Gas			
	ESB			
	Oil			
	Solid fuel			
	Rates			
	Telephone landline			
	Mobile 1			
	Mobile 2			
	Mobile 3			
	Broadband			
	Help-in-House			
	Garden/Gardener			

	Expenditure Analysis	What Has Been Spent Monthly €	What Will Be Spent Monthly €	Notes
	Repairs/Renewals			
	Household Alcohol (?)			
	House Insurance			
	Other Insurance Premiums			
	Laundry and Dry-Cleaning (?)			
	TV/Video Rental (?)			
	TV Licence			
	Housekeeping: Food, Cleaning Materials (?)			
	Pet Foods			
	Holiday Home Expenses (?)			
	Toiletries			
	Newspapers/Magazines/ Books (?)			
	Lotto/Betting (?)			
	Medicines (?)			
	Other (specify) (?)			
	Sub-Total			
2.	Personal Expenses			
	Drinks Out (?)			
	Meals Out (?)			
	Snacks (?)			
	Cigarettes/Tobacco (?)			
	Own Clothing and Footwear (?)			

	Expenditure Analysis	What Has Been Spent Monthly €	What Will Be Spent Monthly €	Notes
	Hair and Beauty (?)			
	Spouse's Clothing and Footwear (?)			
	Christmas and Birthday Presents (?)			
	Holidays Including Weekends Away (?)			
	Subscriptions			
	Sports/Hobbies/ Entertainment (?)			
	Health Insurance			
	Pocket Money/ Miscellaneous Expenditure (?)			
	Donations to Charities			
	Travel and Other Personal Expenses (?)			
	Study (?)			
	Work-Related (?)			
	Sub-total (?)			
3.	Children and Grandchildren			
	Babysitter's Fees (?)			
	Clothing and Footwear			
	Education Expenses			
	Pocket Money			
	Other Children's Expenses (?)			
	Sub-Total			

	Expenditure Analysis	What Has Been Spent Monthly €	What Will Be Spent Monthly €	Notes
4.	Cost of Servicing Debt			
	Mortgage on Residence			
	Hire Purchase			
	Bank Loans/Bank Charges			
	Alimony/Maintenance			
	Other Similar Expenses			
	Sub-Total			
5.	Motoring Expenses			
	Car Tax			
	Car Insurance			
	Petrol/Diesel			
	Services and Repairs			
	AA Subscription			
	Other Expenses			
	Depreciation (To calculate the cost of depreciation use 20% of original market value)			
	Sub-Total			
6.	Investments and Life Assurance			
	Life Assurance Premiums			
	Pension Contributions			
	Government Savings Scheme (SSIA)			

	Expenditure Analysis	What Has Been Spent Monthly €	What Will Be Spent Monthly €	Notes
	Building Society Savings			
	Instalment Savings Plan			
	Business Expansion Scheme			
	Other Savings and Investments			
	Sub-Total			
7.	Professional Fees			
	Accountant			
	GP (?)			
	Dentist (?)			
	Optician (?)			
	Osteopath (?)			
	Physiotherapist (?)			
	Solicitor (?)			
	Veterinary Surgeon (?)			
	Other			
	Sub-Total			

Income Less Expenditure Summary

	What I Have Been Getting Monthly after Tax €	What I Will Get Monthly after Tax €	Notes
Income Summary			
Earned Income – PAYE			
Earned Income – Private			
Bonus/Commission/Fees/ Overtime			
Rental Income			
Investment Income			
Dividend Income			
Jobseeker's Benefit/ Allowance			
Old-Age Pension (Social Welfare)			
Pension			
Child Benefit			
Other Income Including Cash (detail)			
Total income: (a)			

	What Has Been Spent Monthly €	What Will Be Spent Monthly €	Notes
Expenditure – Summary			
Housekeeping Expenses			
Personal Expenses			
Children and Grandchildren			
Cost of Servicing Debts			
Motoring Expenses			
Investment and Life Assurance			
Professional Fees			
Total Expenditure: (b)			
Income Less Expenditure: (a-b)			

Appendix 2
Financial Snapshot

What I Owe Credit Provider	Balance Owing	Term Remaining	Interest Rate	Fixed or Variable Rate	Monthly Repayments	Annual Repayments
Mortgage						
Credit Card						
Bank Term-Loan						
Car Lease						
Credit Union						
Overdraft						
Tax Liability						
Total (a)						

What I Own (Liquid Assets)	Balance or Value	Term	Interest Rate	Fixed or Variable
Bank				
Building Society				
Tracker Bond				
Shares				
Total (b)				

What I Own (Fixed Assets)	Value	Net Equity	* Cash Now Value (d)	Loan to Value LTV
House				
Cars				
Investment Bonds				
Pension Fund				
Total (c)				

Assets				
Total (b) + (c)				
Less (a)				
Net Assets				

Available Cash (b) + (d)				

* Note: the Cash Now Value (d) is an estimate of the fire-sale value of your assets if you had to sell them quickly. Be careful when calculating the value of investments, as these have fallen significantly. There may also be break costs associated with withdrawing money from some deposits – such as tracker bonds and short-term investments – so adjust for these.

Appendix 3
Statement of Affairs

	Assets (What I Own)	€
	Cash	
	Deposits (Bank/Building Society/Credit Union)	
	Guaranteed Investments	
	Equity-based investments	
	Cash Value Savings Policies	
A	Total Liquid Assets	
	Pension	
	Investment Properties	
	Business Assets/Net Asset Value	
	Other Realisable Assets	
B	Total Invested Assets	
	Principal Private Residence (Family Home)	
	Other Personal Assets	
C	Total Assets (A+B)	

	Liabilities (What I Owe)	€
	Bank Overdraft	
	Credit Cards	
	Short-term Debt (1-10 years)	
	Long-term Debt (10 years+)	
	Home Mortgage	
D	Total Liabilities	
E	Net Worth (C-D)	

Note: under Liquid Assets, include funds that you can quickly cash in or redeem. Some medium-term investments have guaranteed capital but if you cash them in early they will be worth less. Include this encashment value under Liquid Assets and the difference between it and guaranteed maturity value under Invested Assets.

Appendix 4
Annual Bill Budget Estimator

Item	Amount €	Notes
Car Insurances		
Car Service		
Car Tax		
House Insurance		
Health Insurance		
Heating Oil/Gas/Solid Fuel		
Electricity		
TV Licence		
Telephone		
Total Bills for the year		
Overdraft Limit (Total ÷ 2)		
Add Interest (Total Bills ÷ 2 x 6%)		
Total Outlay		
Monthly Standing Order (Outlay ÷ 12)		

Note: To estimate your overdraft requirement divide the total for the bills by two. The assumption is that at worst half your bills will arrive in one month, which is unlikely to happen. The interest estimate is to allow for any interest charged on overdrawn balances and fees.

Appendix 5
Specimen Letters to Lenders

Below is an initial letter that can be sent to all your creditors as soon as you realise that you are going to have a problem with repayments.

[Insert your address here]
[Insert date here]

[Insert name of creditor here]
Re Account No: [Insert your account number here]

Dear Sir/Madam
I am writing to you regarding the above account.
The purpose of this letter is to inform you that I am currently experiencing financial difficulties and am in the process of trying to resolve them.
I am at present assessing my full financial situation and working out how much I can pay to each of my creditors, taking into account all my living expenses and commitments.
While I am undertaking this process, it would be of immense help to me if you would put a hold on any action being taken to recover this debt, also if you would suspend any interest and other charges currently being added to this account.
May I take this opportunity to thank you in advance for your cooperation.
Yours faithfully

_____

[Insert your name here]

Below is a letter of offer to a creditor. A completed income and expenditure sheet should accompany this letter.

[Insert your address here]
[Insert date here]

[Insert name of creditor here]
Re Account No: [Insert your account number here]

Dear Sir/Madam

Further to our recent correspondence, I am writing to advise you that I have now completed a full assessment of my current financial situation taking into account all my living expenses and commitments.

As a result I am now putting forward an offer of € per week/month as being realistic in my current circumstances. Should circumstances improve to the extent where I can increase this offer, I will contact you immediately.

In the meantime, I hope that this proposal will be acceptable to you. I would be grateful if you would suspend any interest and other charges being added to the account in order to help me resolve my difficulties within the shortest possible period.

I look forward to hearing from you.

Yours faithfully

[Insert your name here]

These letters are reproduced courtesy of MABS (Money Advice and Budgeting Service) and can also be downloaded from www.mabs.ie.

Appendix 6
Specimen Cashflow Budget

(See overleaf)

Note: the Running Balance calculation begins with your opening overdraft account and credit-card balances. In this case the figure is -€10,000 and the budget shows that at the end of the year the figure will have risen to −€26,330.

		€	1 €	2 €	3 €
Income	Net Salary		7000	7000	7000
	Social Welfare				
	Rent				
	Other				
A	Sub Total		7000	7000	7000
Lump sum	Bonus				
	Commission				
	Tax Rebate				
	Other				
B	Sub-total		0	0	0
A+B	Total Income		7000	7000	7000
Living Expenses	Food		1200	1200	1200
	Heating				
	Electricity		150	150	150
	Clothing		300	300	300
	Transport		400	400	400
	Education				
	Childcare		1200	1200	1200
	House Insurance				
	Car Insurance				
	Car Tax				
	Health Insurance		110	110	110
	Telephone		150	150	150
	TV		50	50	50
	Licence Fees				
	Local Authority			220	
	Building Management				
	Other (List)				
C	Sub Total		3560	3780	3560
Lifestyle	Entertainment		800	800	800
	Holidays				
	Leisure		400	400	400
	Other				
	Cigarettes		270	270	270
D	Sub Total		1470	1470	1470
Debt repayment	Mortgage		1200	1200	1200
	Other Mortgage				
	Car Loan		750	750	750
	Credit Union				
	Other Loans		250	250	250
E	Sub Total		2200	2200	2200
C+D+E	Total Spending		7230	7450	7230
	Total Income		7000	7000	7000
	Less Total Spending		7230	7450	7230
	Savings + Borrowing -		-230	-450	-230
	Running Balance	-10000	-10230	-10680	-10910

4	5	6	7	8	9	10	11	12
€	€	€	€	€	€	€	€	€
7000	7000	7000	7000	7000	7000	7000	7000	7000
7000	7000	7000	7000	7000	7000	7000	7000	7000
				5000				
			1200					
0	0	0	1200	5000	0	0	0	0
7000	7000	7000	8200	12000	7000	7000	7000	7000
1200	1200	1200	1200	1200	1200	1200	1200	1200
600		600		600				
225	225	225	225	225	225	150	150	150
300	300	300	300	300	300	300	300	300
400	400	400	400	400	400	400	400	400
1200	1200	1200	1200	1200	1200	1200	1200	1200
600				750				
		1000			600			
800				400				
110	110	110	110	110	110	110	110	110
150	150	150	150	150	150	150	150	150
50	50	50	50	50	50	50	50	50
		150						
5635	3635	5385	3635	5385	4235	3560	3560	3560
800	800	800	800	800	800	800	800	800
	5000						8000	
400	400	400	400	400	400	400	400	400
270	270	270	270	270	270	270	270	270
1470	6470	1470	1470	1470	1470	1470	9470	1470
1200	1200	1200	1200	1200	1200	1200	1200	1200
750	750	750	750	750	750	750	750	750
250	250	250	250	250	250	250	250	250
2200	2200	2200	2200	2200	2200	2200	2200	2200
9305	12305	9055	7305	9055	7905	7230	15230	7230
7000	7000	7000	8200	12000	7000	7000	7000	7000
9305	12305	9055	7305	9055	7905	7230	15230	7230
-2305	-5305	-2055	895	2945	-905	-230	-8230	-230
-13215	-18520	-20575	-19680	-16735	-17640	-17870	-26100	-26330

Appendix 7
A Summary of the IBF Voluntary Code
on Mortgage Arrears

Lenders recognise the need to distinguish between borrowers who are genuinely unable to pay – because of changed circumstances – and those who could pay some/all of the arrears but will not. All genuine cases will be handled sympathetically and positively by the lender, with the objective at all times of assisting the borrower to meet his/her obligations.

As each case of mortgage arrears is unique and needs to be treated differently, lenders will adopt flexible procedures for the handling of arrears cases, aimed at assisting the borrower as far as possible in his/her particular circumstances.

As soon as an arrears situation develops, the lender will communicate promptly and clearly with the borrower to establish in the first instance why the repayment schedule has not been adhered to and, secondly, how the situation may be rectified. It is in the interests of both the lender and the borrower to address a 'missed payment situation' as speedily and as effectively as circumstances allow. Failure to do so could give rise to a more serious arrears problem with negative consequences for both parties: for the lender, amongst other things greater difficulty in normalising the repayment situation; for the borrower, accumulating arrears that will affect his/her credit rating and give rise to the risk of losing his/her home. Where the arrears situation continues, the lender will continue in its endeavours to make contact with the borrower. This can be by way of further correspondence, telephone contact or a meeting with the borrower.

Once contact has been established, and assuming cooperation from the borrower, a plan for clearing the mortgage arrears can be developed that is consistent with the interests of both the lender and the borrower. All viable options open to the borrower will be examined during which consideration will be given to his/her repayment capacity, previous payment history and the equity remaining in the property.

If a third repayment is missed, the lender may issue a formal demand. With the issue of a formal demand for either the full amount due on foot of the mortgage or for possession of the property, the borrower will have been advised in writing of the following:

- the total amount of arrears;
- where applicable, any excess interest (expressed as a rate or an amount) that may continue to be charged and the basis on which this will be charged; and/or any charges that may be payable
- advice regarding the consequences of failing to respond – namely, the potential for legal proceedings and loss of his/her property – together with an estimate of the costs to the borrower of such proceedings.
- Where the arrears situation persists, the lender reserves the right to enforce the mortgage agreement

As each arrears situation is different, the lender will examine each on its individual merits and the outcome is very likely to differ as a result. They will take into consideration the borrower's overall indebtedness in establishing their ability to repay. This will include full details of household income and expenditure, as advised by the borrower. They will explore with the borrower one or more of the following alternative repayment measures:

- an arrangement on arrears could be entered into, whereby the amount of monthly repayment may be changed, as appropriate, to help address the arrears situation.
- deferring payment of all or part of the instalment repayment for a period might be appropriate where, for example, there is a temporary shortfall of income.
- extending the term of the mortgage could be considered in the case of a repayment loan – although this may not make a significant difference to the monthly repayments.
- changing the type of the mortgage might be appropriate if this could give rise to a reduction in the level of monthly mortgage outgoings (i.e. mortgage and related assurance payments).
- capitalising the arrears and interest could arise where there is insufficient capacity over the short term to clear the arrears but where repayment capacity exists to repay the capitalised balance over the remaining term of the mortgage. This measure will be considered only where a pattern of repayment has been established and where sufficient equity exists.

The appropriateness of these measures will be determined by the factors of each individual arrears case. The borrower should be advised to take appropriate independent advice.

Whichever of the options outlined may be pursued, the lender will provide the borrower with a clear explanation of the alternative repayment arrangement that is being agreed, together with details of any additional interest or administration charges that may arise.

The lender will continue to monitor the repayment arrangement.

The lender will advise the borrower that it is in their interests to ensure that their income is being maximised and a budgeted approach to expenditure maintained. Where circumstances warrant it, consideration will be given to referring the borrower for guidance to his/her local Money Advice and Budgeting Service (MABS) or appropriate alternative. At the borrower's request and with the borrower's written consent, the lender will liaise with a third party nominated by the borrower.

Where appropriate, the borrower will be made aware of other options such as trading down, voluntary sale or alternative refinancing through another lender.

Resources

Advertising Standards Authority of Ireland

This is a voluntary self-regulating association of advertising practitioners, which deals with complaints about standards of advertising. There are voluntary codes of standards, for instance on sales promotion practice, and you can complain about breaches of those standards.

www.asai.ie; 01-6608766

AWARE

A national voluntary organisation providing support for people suffering from depression and their families. The organisation undertakes to create a society where people with depression are understood and supported, are free from stigma and have access to a broad range of appropriate therapies to enable them to reach their full potential.

Services include support groups nationwide, a loCall Helpline open 365 days a year (both services available to individuals with depression and also family members and friends), Beat the Blues, a secondary school awareness programme, depression awareness and information talks and seminars and a free information service.

www.aware.ie; Lo Call 1890-30-33-02

Book

Andrew McCann. *Know Your Rights: A Simple Guide to Social and Civic Entitlements in Ireland*. Dublin: Blackhall Publishing, 2007.

A handy, easy-to-use guide for all ages and an essential reference book for any household.

Citizens Information Board

This organisation has an excellent public website chock-full of information on all aspects of living and working in Ireland. A great starting point, with links to government and private-sector websites.

www.citizensinformation.ie; Lo-call 1890-777-121

Commission for Communications Regulation (ComReg)

ComReg has two sites. Its consumer site is a great source of information on telephone, mobile, internet and postal services, including tips, advice and lots of free stuff.

www.askcomreg.ie

It also provides a cost comparison website allowing people to compare the costs of different packages.

www.callcosts.ie; 1890-229-669

Consumers' Association of Ireland (CAI)

An independent non-for-profit association working to make sure that people's needs as consumers of goods and services are given higher priority

www.consumerassociation.ie; 01-4978600

Data-Protection Commissioner

You have a fundamental right to privacy and to access and correct data about yourself. Those who keep data about you have to comply with strict protection principles.

www.dataprotection.ie; Lo-Call 1890-252-231

Department of Social and Family Affairs

This department is responsible for the delivery of a range of social-insurance and social-assistance schemes including provision for unemployment, illness, maternity, caring, widowhood, retirement and old age.

www.welfare.ie.

Check telephone directory and department website for a full list of local offices and contact numbers.

Financial Regulator

The Financial Regulator is the body that regulates financial service firms and aims to help people make informed decisions about their personal finances.

Its consumer website is full of product guides and advice on consumer financial services and a good start for finding out more about managing your finances.

www.itsyourmoney.ie; Lo-Call 1890-77-77-77

Financial Services Ombudsman

A statutory body that deals independently with unresolved complaints from consumers and their individual dealings with financial-service providers. Check out its site for your rights as a consumer of financial services and for advice about how to complain.

www.financialombudsman.ie; Lo-Call 1890-88-20-90

Free Legal Advice Centres (FLAC)

FLAC is an independent human-rights organisation dedicated to the realisation of equal access to justice for all. To this end it campaigns on a range of legal issues but also offers some basic free services to the public.
www.flac.ie; 01-8745690

Food Safety Authority of Ireland

A regulatory authority focused on the enforcement of food safety legislation and dedicated to protecting public health and consumer interests in food safety and hygiene.
www.fsai.ie; 01-817-1300

Health Insurance Authority

Regulates the private health-insurance market. Check out your rights on its website.
www.hia.ie; 01-4060080

Irish Bankers' Federation

The IBF Voluntary Code on Mortgage Arrears can be found on www.ibf.ie

Legislation

Copies of legislation and regulations covering financial service providers can be downloaded from a number of government sites. The main sources are the Consumer Credit Act and the Consumer Protection Code. Your best port of call is the Financial Regulator's sites:
www.ifsra.ie and www.itsyourmoney.ie

Money Advice and Budgeting Service (MABS)

A national, free, confidential and independent service for people in debt or in danger of getting into debt. Through its national network of offices MABS provides *free* debt counselling services.

Good site full of advice on how to manage debts.

www.mabs.ie; Lo-Call 1890-283-438

National Consumer Agency (NCA)

A statutory body with the aim of defending consumer interests and embedding a robust consumer culture in Ireland. Its mandate is to protect and promote consumer rights. It has an excellent website full of consumer information and guides.

www.consumerconnect.ie and

www.consumerproperty.ie; Lo-Call 1890-432-432

Office of the Information Commissioner

This office monitors the operation of Freedom of Information Act which gives people the right to access information from public bodies

www.oic.gov.ie; Lo-Call 1890-223-030

Office of the Ombudsman

This office investigates complaints about the administrative actions of government departments, the HSE, local authorities and An Post.

www.ombudsman.gov.ie; Lo-Call 1890-22-30-30

Pensions Board

A statutory body regulating occupational pension schemes and PRSAs, protecting the interests of pension-scheme members and encouraging pension provision. The board's site contains a lot of information on pensions in Ireland. www.pensionsboard.ie; Lo-Call 1890-656-565

Pensions Ombudsman

The role of this office is to investigate complaints of financial loss due to maladministration and disputes of fact or law in relation to occupational pension schemes and PRSAs. www.pensionsombudsman.ie; 01-6471650

Revenue Commissioners

The Revenue Commissioners have a good site full of information on all aspects of personal and business taxation. Can take some getting used to but worth the effort. This information is also available from Citizens Information Board, as above.
www.revenue.ie.

Check the telephone directory and the Revenue website for a full list of local offices and contact numbers.

Safe Food

This is a North-South body promoting food safety in Ireland. Interesting website with some handy guides and reference material.
www.safefood.eu; 1850-404-567

Sustainable Energy Ireland

This government body is a good source for information and tips on using energy wisely. Check out the 'Your Home' section.

www.SEI.ie; 1850-37-66-66

Threshold National Housing Organisation

A not-for-profit organisation with a regional network of offices that helps people with housing difficulties. Its site provides useful information on tenants' rights and landlords' obligations.

www.threshold.ie; 01-6786310